A Long Hot Soak

A Long Hot Soak

Over Fifty Stories to Warm the Heart and Inspire the Spirit

INTRODUCED BY DON MACLEAN

COMPILED BY CHRIS GIDNEY

HarperCollins*Publishers*

HarperCollins*Publishers*
77–85 Fulham Palace Road, London W6 8JB
www.**fireandwater**.com

Stories previously published by Guideposts Books
This compilation first published in Great Britain in 2001
by HarperCollins*Religious*

5 7 9 10 8 6

A catalogue record for this book is
available from the British Library.

ISBN 0 00 274056 7

Printed in Great Britain by
Clays Ltd, St Ives plc

CONTENTS

Foreword by Chris Gidney ix
Introduction by Don Maclean MBE xi

1. Seeing Friendship Win Through 1

Something Old, Something New *Anita Gogno* 3
The Swans and the Goose *Charlotte Edwards* 5
The Handshake *Ben Purcell* 8
Bald Love *Arnie Shein* 11
A Secret Shame *Adele Martin* 12
A Nice Trick *Connie Wells* 16
Conflicting Emotions *Anne Lawler* 17
Frankie *Victor Wheeler* 22
Point of View *Linda Neukrug* 25
Newsnight *Manuel Almada* 26
Man's Best Friend *Carter Allen* 28
Blooming Love *Connie Kelton* 31

2. Making Success out of Failure 33

A Pearl of Great Value *Marcia Evans* 35
The Rescue *Ernest Poston* 40
A Picture of Triumph *Marie Gaskin* 44
Don't be Frightened of Failure *Austin Pardue* 49
Exploding Hope *Ethel Stewart* 52

Full Circle *Ike Keay* 53
Taking 'no' for an Answer *Ben Patterson* 59
Hope Beyond the Flames *Robert Wheeler* 61
A Rusty Bolt *Daniel Schantz* 66

3. Observing Victory Through Loss 69

A Change of Heart *Jeri Boley* 71
To Love the Rain *Aletha Lindstrom* 75
Remembering Michael *Frank Bianco* 79
Hope has a Face *Kenneth Culver* 83
A Story of Life and Death *Jenny Wade* 88
The Midnight Bell *Judy Armstrong* 94
The Grant of Time *Ruth Boellstorff* 96
The Wall *Duery Felton* 100
The Chair that Sang *Melissa Young* 102
Lessons from Lois *Carol Kuykendall* 104

4. When Trust Overcomes Doubt 109

Man without a Past *Stan Peterson* 111
The Yellow Kite *Beverly Newman* 116
The Solution *Joe Barbera* 120
A Future and a Hope *Lloyd Ogilvie* 122
Death was my Biggest Fear *Bob Morgan* 127
A Sense of Humour *Brenda Wilbee* 129
Once in a Million *Frank Tripp* 130
The Woman from Nowhere *Laura Sowers* 132
Tough Love *Gordon Dobson* 135

5. Discovering Healing Through Sickness 141

A Dreadful Decision *Dr Kenneth Swan* 143
Angels Among Us *Susan Grezel* 148
The Highest Gifts *Charles Allen* 150
Heavenly Truths *Adam DePrince* 155
It's What You Have That Counts *Linda Williams* 158

A Gift at Springtime *Beverly Ruth* 163
The Woman Who Couldn't Cry *Susan Holliday* 168
The Unseen Visitor *Lori White* 174

6. On Conquering the Hurdles 179

Out of the Shadows *Ellen Lawrence* 181
Keeping a Promise *Sam Stoneburner* 186
Night of the Storm *Stuart Reininger* 191
Sound Sleeper *Virginia Seters* 196
Snow Bridge Rescue *Jim Smith* 198
Ten Minutes of Terror *Don Clendenin* 203
Voyage of Hope *Thomas Fleming* 207
Wrestling with Alligators *Robert Green* 212
True Confession *Paul Galanti* 216

Useful Addresses 219

FOREWORD

by Chris Gidney

Co-incidence or God-incidence? We have all been subject to moments of panic and fear where for an instant we are not quite sure what to do, or which way to turn. For some, it is a major event like an accident or bereavement; for others, a heavy worry that gnaws away deep inside. It is often at these critical moments when an internal instinct suddenly takes over. Some put this down to human resourcefulness and others to spiritual guidance. The following stories of real people facing different life events are true, yet most of them claim that an unseen, guiding hand was there just when they needed it. Read them, be inspired, encouraged and stirred, and ultimately judge for yourself.

INTRODUCTION

by Don Maclean MBE

Don Maclean, star of numerous television and stage shows, is certainly a high-flyer. Not just because he has been the presenter of Britain's BBC Radio 2's most prestigious Sunday morning programme for more than ten years and gets to travel around the world, but because he actually flies his own plane.

An American official was recently quoted as saying, 'Flying is no more dangerous than going to the bathroom.' I remember thinking, 'Yeah, but if you slip off the loo you don't fall three thousand feet.' Having said that, there's little chance of a light aircraft falling out of the sky. I'm fastidious when it comes to pre-take-off checks and I always get comprehensive weather reports, so what can go wrong?

The greatest hazard for general aviation pilots in the UK is weather – how, in such a small country, can the weather vary so much? Low cloud is a pilot's nightmare. A cloud may look lovely and white and fluffy but inside one it's like a coal cellar at midnight. Airliners fly above cloud; small, unpressurized aircraft don't have that option. Once in cloud the pilot can no longer fly visually – he has to rely entirely on instruments, gluing his eyes to the altimeter, the air speed indicator and, most importantly, the artificial horizon. Though I practise flying on instruments regularly, it was not my expertise but rather my reliance on another expert that was to get me through that pilot's nightmare.

Together with my friend and fellow pilot, Bill Ballard, I set off for Edinburgh at 7 a.m. on a fine April morning. The sky was clear at

Wellesbourne and the forecast for Edinburgh was giving cloud broken at 2000 ft. It looked good; we should be on the ground by 9 a.m. at the latest. Travelling at 140 m.p.h. soon gobbles up the distance and is invaluable when showbiz demands that I'm in two places on the same day. The trip was uneventful with Bill and I alternating duties, one flying while the other took charge of the radio and the navigation. We crossed through the Newcastle overhead at 3000 ft and set course for St Abb's Head. The sky was clear; in the distance, we could see the sun sparkling off the surface of the sea. At SAB we turned on to a heading of 270 due west, which would bring us straight into Edinburgh.

Almost immediately we flew into a wall of cloud that reached right down to the surface. The weather forecast we'd obtained two hours earlier had promised a 2000-ft cloud base at Edinburgh, so we therefore assumed this to be isolated weather. Bill was flying; I contacted our destination on the radio.

'Edinburgh approach, good morning, this is Gulf Delta Oscar November India.'

'G-DONI passes your message.'

'Thank you, sir. G-DONI, AA5B, inbound to you from Wellesbourne via SAB. Thirty miles to run to the field, two thousand feet, India Mike – flying on instruments – estimate field at time zero five.' There was an unusually long pause before the controller replied, 'G-NI confirms two thousand feet IFR.'

'Affirm, G-NI,' I replied.

'Climb now to four thousand feet and report level,' said the controller. Oh heck, instead of clearing us to descend, he was sending us further up into the clag.

'Level at four thousand feet, G-NI,' I reported. Up here the cloud was so thick I could just about see the wing tips.

'G-NI cloud base at Edinburgh now two hundred feet, repeat two hundred feet, we cannot accept you. What are your intentions?' I was captain of the aircraft, I was in the left-hand seat, and I had to make an immediate decision.

'Request Glasgow's weather, sir.' The weather at Glasgow was slightly better, cloud base 800 ft.

'Request divert to Glasgow, sir.'

'G-NI understood. Route to Uniform Whisky [a navigation beacon] not below four thousand feet.'

'Wilco,' I replied, and gave Bill the heading.

By now he'd been flying on instruments for some time and was feeling the tension. I knew it was essential for us both to keep calm but would Glasgow accept us? We spent an anxious few moments knowing that the Edinburgh controller was contacting Glasgow ATC by phone.

'G-NI Glasgow will accept you, change frequency now to 119.10.' I did so.

'Glasgow, good morning, G-DONI with you requesting SRA [Surveillance Radar Approach].' Now we had to do exactly what the Glasgow controller told us to do with extreme precision.

'G-NI, make your heading 260 and descend to two thousand feet.' By now Bill was getting disoriented and finding it difficult to maintain height and heading. Things got worse when the controller said that he also could not accept us inbound, due to worsening weather. Something had to be done.

'Unable to divert sir, insufficient fuel.' I knew that the controller would now do all he could to get us on the ground.

'G-NI, report your fuel endurance.'

'Fifteen minutes,' I replied.

'Confirm one five minutes.'

'Affirm, sir,' I said.

'Climb now to five thousand feet and report level.' Heck, he's sending us further up into the clag.

'I have control,' I said to Bill. 'You have control,' he repeated, and immediately took over radio and navigation.

'G-NI level at five thousand,' said Bill. The Controller gave me heights and headings for the next fifteen minutes, which I followed meticulously despite experiencing severe turbulence in the cloud. He descended us 500 ft at a time.

I can't tell you how I felt, watching the altimeter as I descended through 1000 ft and still not seeing the ground, but you can imagine how I felt when we actually broke cloud at 750 ft over Glasgow City Centre. Now was arguably the most dangerous bit. Having been flying on instruments I was now flying visually, my relief was palpable but

I knew I mustn't relax. Although it was ten-thirty in the morning, it was extremely dark and the rain was pouring down, the propeller wash pushed the rain to either side keeping my windscreen clear.

'G-NI runway 28, position for straight-in approach, call field in sight.'

Despite the fact that all the runway lights were on, we were a mere one mile from the threshold before either of us saw it. I landed too fast and too far down the runway but I was just glad to have tarmac, not fresh air, under me. I learned later that three airliners were put into a holding pattern to allow us priority. We did have fuel left but not much. As I taxied in I thanked God for the competence and calmness of the controller and whispered aloud the words of Psalm 27: 'The Lord is my light and my salvation, of what shall I be afraid?'

Sitting in my cockpit, with sweat pouring down my face, I reflected on how often life is just like this. Sometimes the speed at which we live our lives can cause great exhilaration or deep concern. When we feel we are flying on our own, in a position of great danger, and in unknown territory, we have to rely on faith, determination, and others to guide us through the fog of life.

A Long Hot Soak contains the stories of real people who found that they had the ability to overcome whatever life threw at them with an inner strength they never knew existed. Many acknowledge a power bigger than themselves that ultimately gave them the strength to cope.

Most of these stories are new to me, and minor details and some names have been changed in order to protect the privacy of the individuals concerned, but they all contain essential ingredients which I have discovered to be vital in my own life: Faith, Friendship and Hope. These people are no different from you and I, and what they have achieved we can achieve too. So, read on, and be inspired.

Don Maclean

1

SEEING FRIENDSHIP WIN THROUGH

A friendship should be tended and cared for just like a garden.

Connie Kelton

SOMETHING OLD, SOMETHING NEW

by Anita Gogno

An old ring revives a friendship.

A few years ago, my husband Charlie and I had marital problems. Growing family responsibilities and financial worries took a toll on us, and we began arguing frequently, often late into the night. Even going out together for dinner was strained and full of forced conversation.

However, neither of us could take the step that would end our eleven-year marriage and bring heartbreak to our three young children. Deep down we knew we still loved each other, so we pledged to work it out.

The year that followed was hard. We discovered how Charlie and I had grown neglectful about expressing ourselves, and how for too long we had let small differences and disappointments build between us. We had stored up reserves of anger and resentment that pushed us far apart. Through countless discussions, we began to close the gulf. The more honest we were, the closer we became.

When I felt we were reaching solid ground, I asked my husband to give me an 'eternity ring'. I had bought the advertising hype hook, line and sinker: '*Show her you'd marry her all over again.*' It was not so much the ring I wanted; it was the reassurance I thought it would bring.

We went shopping on a beautiful summer day, my birthday. We left the kids with their grandparents and had a leisurely lunch before walking hand in hand along a row of jeweller's shops. Finally I found a ring I liked. While waiting for it to be adjusted, the jeweller took my left hand and peered at my engagement ring. 'May I clean it for you?' he asked.

Charlie hunched over me and leaned on the glass case. 'It really doesn't sparkle like it used to,' he said, as I slipped the ring off my finger. A few minutes later the jeweller was back. The ring shone like new!

On the drive home, I didn't take my eyes off it. I forgot all about the eternity ring. I just couldn't believe how this old ring suddenly sparkled the way it had the day Charlie gave it to me. I had taken it for granted these last years, but with a little polish it could still make my heart beat fast.

And that's the way it is with a marriage. You have to work at keeping it polished and new, or else the grime of the passing years will hide the joy. I put my hand on the seat between us and spread my fingers. Charlie covered my hand with his. As we pulled into the driveway, I said a silent prayer of thanks for being able to see the sparkle in something old when I thought I needed something new.

THE SWANS AND THE GOOSE

by Charlotte Edwards

My friend was on her feet with one unbelieving hand against her mouth.

On the Eastern Shore of Maryland, where we live, the gentle waters run in and out like fingers slimming at the tips. They curl into the smaller creeks and coves like tender palms.

The Canada geese know this, as do the fat white swans and the ducks that ride an inch above the waves of Chesapeake Bay as they skim their way into harbour. In the autumn they come home for the winter by the thousands.

In hunting season the air is filled with the sound of guns. The shores are scattered with blinds; the creeks and rivers with duck and goose decoys. The swans are a different matter entirely. Protected by law, they move towards the shores in a stately glide, their tall heads proud and unafraid. They lower their long necks deep into the water, where their strong beaks dig through the river bottoms for food. Between the arrogant swans and the prolific geese there is indifference, almost a disdain.

Once or twice each year, snow and sleet move into the area. When this happens, if the river is at its narrowest, or the creek shallow, there is a freeze that hardens the water to ice.

It was on such a morning near Oxford, Maryland, that a friend of mine set the breakfast table and poured the coffee beside the huge window that looked out from her home on the Tred Avon River. Across the waters beyond the dock, snow laced the rim of the shore in white. For a moment she stood quietly, looking at what the night's storm had painted.

Suddenly she leaned forward and peered close to the frosted window. 'It really is!' she cried aloud. 'There's a goose out there. She reached to the bookcase and pulled out a pair of binoculars. Into their sights came the figure of a large Canada goose, very still, its wings folded tight to its sides, its feet frozen to the ice.

Then from the dark sky, white against its lacklustre, she saw a line of swans. They moved in their own singular formation, graceful, intrepid and free. They crossed from the west of the broad creek high above the house, moving steadily to the east.

As my friend watched, the leader swung to the right. Then the white string of birds became a white circle. It floated from the top of the sky downwards. At last, as easy as feathers coming to earth, the circle landed on the ice.

My friend was on her feet, with one unbelieving hand against her mouth. As the swans surrounded the frozen goose, she feared that what life he still had might be pecked out by those great swan bills. Instead, amazingly, those bills began to work on the ice. The long necks were lifted and curved down, again and again, as deliberately as a pick swung over the head of a fisherman cutting a free space for his winter rod. It went on for a long time.

At last the goose was rimmed by a narrow margin of ice instead of the entire creek. The swans rose again, following the leader, and hovered in that circle, awaiting the results of their labours.

The goose's head was lifted. Its body pulled. Then the goose was free and standing on the ice. He was moving his big, webbed feet slowly. The swans stayed in the air over him, watching.

Then as if he had cried, 'I cannot fly,' four swans flew down around him. Their powerful beaks scraped the goose's wing from top to bottom, scuttled under its wings and rode up its body, chipping off and melting the ice held in the feathers.

Slowly, as if testing, the goose spread its wings as far as they would go, brought them together, accordion like, and spread them again. When at last the wings reached their full span, the four swans took off and joined the hovering group. They resumed their eastward journey, in perfect, impersonal formation, to a secret destination.

Behind them, rising with incredible speed and joy, the goose moved into the sky. He followed them, flapping double time, until he caught up, until he joined the last of the line, like a small dark child at the end of a crack-the-whip of older boys.

My friend watched them until they disappeared over the tips of the furthest trees. Only then, did she realize that tears were running down her cheeks, and she had no idea as to how long she had been crying.

This is a true story. It happened. I do not try to interpret it. I just think of it in the bad moments, and from it comes a hopeful question: if so for birds, why not for us?

THE HANDSHAKE

by Ben Purcell

The simple touch of a human hand was enough.

At the first stab of dawn a cockerel crowed. For a moment, a cruelly brief moment, I was back at the family farm in Clarkesville, Georgia, with my wife, Anne, slumbering beside me, and our five children snug in their beds down the hall. I could almost feel Anne's sturdy warmth. As the sun pierced the tiny, barred window and forced open my eyes, I was jerked back to my true surroundings at a North Vietnamese POW camp, 'home' for the three years since I'd been captured during the bloody offensive in February 1968.

I eased into a sitting position on the wooden slab that was my bunk, trying to stretch out the ache in my back. My eye roamed the dingy cell. I knew every inch of it. It was all I knew. Three years of total isolation. I received no word from home, no contact with other prisoners. I'd not even been allowed to write to Anne, though in my heart I spoke to her day and night, praying God would keep her and the children safe and let them know I was surviving.

Survival. I had to keep my mind disciplined. In my thoughts I 'reread' the books from my college literature classes. *Oliver Twist*, *Crime and Punishment*, *Of Human Bondage*. One guard reminded me a bit of Henry Fonda, and that got me projecting my favourite movies on a bright, wide internal screen. I watched *My Darling Clementine* again and again, slowing down and replaying favourite scenes. Also, I never strayed from my greatest comfort. Daily, I read Scripture – not that I was actually permitted a Bible. But deep in my mind I read and reread the pages from Sunday school until they were smudged creased and tattered.

Still there were moments I thought I might snap. Worse than any torture, the sheer agony of solitude, of being unable to experience the simplest human contact, was what I feared would finally undo me. Somehow I think my captors knew that too.

God, I prayed that morning as I did every morning, please help ease the loneliness. Give me strength to go on. Slipping off my bunk I began my daily routine. I was required to sweep out my cell. I relished the job. It brought order and purpose to the start of my day. As usual, I took my broom and went over every precious foot of floor. When I finished I flicked the small pile of sweepings through a four-inch gap at the bottom of my door into the passageway beyond where some unseen camp trusty would sweep it up for collection.

Suddenly, the little pile was swept briskly back into my cell.

Odd, I thought. Why would he do that? I pushed the pile back out, thinking the trusty had made a mistake. It came right back in. This is deliberate, I realized testily. I swept it out. Again it came back.

Now I was mad. I flicked the rubbish back under the door and got down on my hands and knees. As soon as the broom came towards the gap again, I reached under and grabbed it.

'Khong!' the trusty hissed. Vietnamese for 'no'. He jerked back the broom but I held on, terrier-tight. For a moment we grunted and tussled. His struggling told me he was frightened. If he were caught messing with one of the American POWs he'd be harshly dealt with.

I thought about that. He was, after all, a prisoner, like me. Why get him into any more trouble than what had already landed him in here? So I turned the broom loose. At least that'll teach him a lesson, I thought to myself.

It was curious that I didn't hear him scuffling off. I'd have thought he would have wanted to get away from the crazy American. Instead, there was just his laboured breathing on the other side of the door. I stayed on my knees by the opening, straining for some clue to his behaviour. Finally he was silent. I wasn't even sure he was still there when, to my astonishment, the strangest thing happened. He thrust his thin hand under my cell door. I stepped back. He slapped his palm on the floor, and then offered it to me in the form of a handshake.

I froze. Maybe this was a trick. But something silently whispered reassurance that the man on the other side was trying to reach out to me.

Slowly, I stretched my fingers towards his, almost afraid to touch another human being again in friendship. When I lightly felt his hand he quickly pulled my fingers into his hungry grip. A kind of warm physical music played throughout me, a combustion of feelings that had been trapped for so long. I put my other hand over his, covering our grip. Then he reached under the door and did the same.

It was a dangerous moment, but we let it linger as long as we could. Then quickly we both withdrew our hands.

I never encountered that trusty again, whoever he was – a North Vietnamese civilian, a South Vietnamese soldier? But for a moment we were just two human beings reaching out.

In the remaining two years of my captivity I was sustained by the simple touch of a hand. That one moment of caring human contact that I so desperately needed, that we all need, to go on.

BALD LOVE

by Arnie Shein

Manuel bolted up in bed and looked at them in awe.

I was recuperating from surgery when the nurses wheeled in Manuel, my new room-mate. Before long our hospital room was as busy as a railway station. Thirty-nine-year-old Manuel had made a host of friends since he and his family had moved here from Puerto Rico. Now he seemed to thrive on their constant support and attention. I'm going to be fine, be kept promising them.

Then came bad news. Manuel had cancer. He'd have to undergo radiation therapy and chemotherapy. For Manuel, however, the worst news seemed to be that he would lose his magnificent head of hair.

He was inconsolable. Nothing I said reassured him. It was obvious he had focused all anxiety about his health on a fear of losing his hair. One morning, a few days later, we heard the shuffling of feet outside our door.

A group of Manuel's friends and family led by his five-year-old son, Miguel, marched in. Dumbstruck, Manuel bolted up in bed and looked at them in awe.

They had all shaved their heads.

A SECRET SHAME

by Adele Martin

I could never forgive myself for what I'd done to my best friend.

In the hotel room, I smoothed out the black dress I'd packed for Marcie's funeral. After the plane trip, I was still weak with grief. Carl and I owed our marriage, our happiness, everything we had, to Marcie. There was nothing I could ever do to repay her. And now she was dead.

I grew angry as I showered and dressed, thinking about how she'd died. A drunk high school student had swerved his car into her lane, crashing head-on into her car, killing her. The young driver had walked away unharmed. Unforgivable! Is there no justice in this world? I tugged at the zip on my dress. 'Be gentle,' Marcie would have said, 'you'll rip it.' She was always more patient than I.

As college room-mates, we had hit it off right from the start. We did everything together, including going to chapel. Marcie insisted. She also taught Sunday school and visited the old folks' home every week. I was prepared to put my foot down if she got too holy with me. But Marcie didn't preach about her faith; she simply put it to use.

One evening during our senior year, we walked back to the dorm after a meeting. 'Guess what?' she said. 'John asked me for a date.'

'John?'

'Mm-hmm.'

I focused on the sidewalk.

'And I said yes!'

He's not right for her, I thought. He doesn't even go to church. 'I hope you have a good time,' I managed to say. The truth was, I'd had a secret crush on John since my first year.

After graduation, I was the Maid of honour in John and Marcie's wedding. I still cared about John, but I figured that once I found someone for myself I'd get over it.

Marcie kept our friendship close. We saw each other as much as ever, usually with John. How could I tell Marcie it was hard for me to be around him? We teased each other and laughed easily. As a popular college football hero, John was no stranger to female attention. He seemed to like it, especially coming from me.

Then one summer a couple of years after their wedding, Marcie called. 'We're going to a beachside bungalow for a whole week,' she said. 'You must come too.' Marcie wouldn't take no for an answer.

About midweek Marcie went into town to see a friend in the hospital. That left John and me alone in the bungalow.

John flopped on to the couch. I kicked off my shoes and sat next to him, bare legs tucked under me. We talked about college days.

'You were the best-looking guy on campus,' I said. John was every bit as handsome now. This is the kind of man I want, I thought. Without actually planning it, I began to play up to him. I felt like I was acting in a movie, and gave not a thought to real-life consequences.

'Want something to eat?' I asked, getting up slowly. When I looked over my shoulder at John, he grabbed my arm and twirled me back on to the couch. I giggled, and then fell silent. Before either of us knew what was happening, we had betrayed Marcie.

Immediately afterwards, it was as though I had awakened from a terrible dream. I felt sick inside. How could you? My conscience raged, as I stumbled into the bathroom.

Somehow I finished out the week, and avoided them afterwards as much as possible. Every time I looked Marcie in the face, my own shame welled up in me.

I began dating a man and we soon married. Marcie was my Matron of honour. It wasn't a happy marriage; we divorced after three years. Marcie stood by me throughout the whole ordeal. The kinder she was to me, the guiltier I felt. You're no good, I told myself. And you're getting what you deserve.

Marcie and John had two children, a boy and a girl, and John started going to church with them. 'It's made my life complete,' Marcie told me, 'he's such a good man.' Only I knew how that portrait was marred. Thanks to me, I reminded myself bitterly.

Their children were teenagers when John developed pancreatic cancer. Within a year, he was dead. Marcie was devastated. At his funeral, Marcie introduced me to Carl, a family friend. I liked him immediately. Three months after our first date, he asked me to marry him. I loved him, and yet I couldn't say yes. I didn't deserve someone as good as Carl.

'He brings out something in you I haven't seen in a long time,' Marcie said to me one day. 'Why aren't you jumping at his offer?'

The weight of the years pressed down on me, and I burst into tears. 'I'm a horrible person,' I sobbed.

'No, Adele,' Marcie said. 'No, you're not.'

'But you don't know. You don't know how I've wronged you!'

As soon as the words passed my lips, I regretted having said them. I clutched my hands to my mouth, waiting for her to ask me what I was talking about. I couldn't tell her. It wasn't fair for me to destroy the memories she had of John.

'But I do know, Adele,' she said, taking me in her arms. 'I've known for a long, long time.'

She can't possibly! Pulling away, I looked into her face, which was full of compassion. Her eyes told me she knew everything. 'After – all these years,' I stammered, 'how could you have kept me as your friend?'

'Because I love you,' she said, 'and John. I didn't want to lose either of you, so I forgave you both.'

I wanted to hug her, but my shame was an almost physical presence separating us, just as it was keeping me from Carl. 'I'm so sorry.'

'I know,' she said. She took my arm and we knelt. I asked God's forgiveness. 'And help her, Lord, to forgive herself,' Marcie added.

That had taken time. But now, as I drove to the church for Marcie's funeral, I thought about the long way I had come since that day she and I had prayed together. Marrying Carl was the best thing I had ever done. My happiness taught me that there's nothing that can't be forgiven.

At Marcie's funeral there was no bitterness spoken by her children for the senseless way she had died. Instead, her daughter told me that she felt sorry for the boy who had killed her mother. 'He will have to carry that memory for the rest of his life,' she said. I knew what it was to carry a heavy burden.

Right there and then I said a prayer for that boy. And the anger I felt towards him left my heart. Maybe that's the true justice in this world, I thought, that we forgive one another. Finally I had found a way to make up to Marcie all she'd done for me.

A NICE TRICK

by Connie Wells

'Antiques'

Lured by a sign saying 'Antiques', my husband and I stopped at a cottage where two elderly ladies ushered us into the living room and served us tea. When we asked to see the antiques, one announced hesitantly, 'We're the antiques!'

'We needed friends,' the other explained. 'But how could we make them? That's when we thought of the antiques sign. Only nice people appreciate lovely things. Remember though, our sign doesn't say, "Antiques for Sale".'

'We've made so many lasting friendships', the other added, 'that we're sure God isn't angry about our little trick!'

CONFLICTING EMOTIONS

by Anne Lawler

Kevin won't even be able to lift his glass to toast them, I said to myself.

It's hard to explain the difficulty I felt when my husband Kevin received an invitation in May 1988 to attend his twenty-fifth class reunion at his old College in Worcester.

'This is great!' Kevin exclaimed. 'It says meals will be in the dining hall and we'll be sleeping in our old dorms. Just like the old days! And there'll be a dinner dance and a five-mile race up and down the Hill! I can hardly wait!'

Kevin reeled off this list of activities with boyish enthusiasm as he sat in his motorized wheelchair, while I was thinking, 'There's no way we can do this.'

Kevin suffers from advanced multiple sclerosis. He is severely impaired. His old college is built on Mount Saint James – the Hill, they call it. Everywhere you turn there are steep gradients or huge flights of steps. We'd be constantly calling attention to ourselves asking for help with Kevin's wheelchair, or having everybody wait for us. Furthermore, Kevin would have to be spoon-fed, in full view of everyone in the dining hall, and would need assistance in the men's room.

It wasn't only that I was hesitant to subject him, and myself, to that kind of embarrassment, I was sure we'd make the others feel uncomfortable as well. We would end up being a nuisance and a burden to everyone on what was supposed to be a fun weekend.

Kevin's old classmates, Charlie Buchta, Denny Golden and Pete O'Connor, were all healthy, vigorous men in their prime. Well-meaning as they are, healthy people can inadvertently be thoughtless around the disabled. His friends would be swapping stories about their old athletic triumphs and their current business deals and successes. Kevin won't even be able to lift his glass to toast them, I said to myself.

When he was healthy, Kevin had been successful in both sports and business. In school and college he had run on the track and cross-country teams. Later, he owned his own estate brokerage firm, built a shopping centre and taught college courses in estate management.

Even when the onset of his MS caused slurred speech and loss of balance, Kevin kept working. By 1986 he could no longer walk. Fatigue and loss of muscle control took an added toil. Finally, he had to stop working. Yet Kevin bore it all with a kind of cheerful optimism and an unshakable faith in God.

The day came when we had to accept social security help, but thanks to a modest inheritance, we already owned a beautiful home, our three daughters were in college, and I was completing my master's degree in social work so that I could contribute to our income. We had never been in real want, yet, in spite of our blessings, there were always problems for us as an MS family. This invitation to Kevin's class reunion was one of them. We kept putting off our decision about attending. The weeks passed into June, and the reunion weekend.

'I don't think we can do it after all,' Kevin announced one day, trying to sound casual. 'It'll be too much.' We sent our regrets.

Getting to church was always difficult, but on the weekend of the reunion we made it a point. At coffee hour afterwards everybody clustered around Kevin and made a fuss over him, which I think helped keep his mind off things. When we returned to our house Denny and Monica Golden were waiting. They were on their way home early from the reunion. I was surprised. It was really considerate of them to stop by. Kind of painful too, hearing what fun it had been.

'How did your keynote speech go on Saturday?' I asked Denny, a bit too brightly.

'Really terrific!' he replied, and then added, 'Anne, we talked about you and Kevin from the platform. I told our classmates how courageous we think you guys are and how much you would have liked to come.'

All the while I was thinking that again we had been put in the position of being a burden.

'We didn't want to be a burden on all of you,' I replied, not looking at him.

'A burden?' he exclaimed. 'No way! Monica, can you believe these guys? Hey, it would have been our pleasure to have lent a hand if you had needed it!'

Turning to Kevin he said, 'Kev, we have a gift from the class to you. Read some of these. You'll see.' He handed Kevin a book of signatures with messages from almost every couple that attended.

Oh, my gosh! I thought, going crimson-faced, recalling my ideas about well-intentioned but thoughtless people. Here they were, thinking about Kevin the whole time! 'Hon, listen to this!' and Kevin read: 'Dear Kev, thinking of you. Really wish you could have been here!' And there were more. His face was radiant. I could have cried.

We didn't have a thing in the refrigerator, so we went out for lunch. Denny helped me get Kevin and his wheelchair into the car, then out again at the restaurant, and then in again when we went home. In the days that followed we began getting calls and notes from his classmates, all saying how much they missed him. That autumn a bunch of guys came up to see their old college play once more. Kevin would have loved being with the gang and yelling at the top of his lungs. But, though we're close to the college, we couldn't attend the game.

This time we did get to an after-game party. When we got ready to leave there were five strong friends to wrestle Kevin's wheelchair into the car, amidst a lot of good-natured joshing. When they drove us home and helped Kevin into the house, Denny and Peter and the others pulled me aside. 'Uh, Anne,' Denny began, 'when we stopped by after the reunion, Monica and I realized what a struggle it is getting Kev into the car. So we came up with an idea. How would you guys feel if the class bought Kevin a van specially equipped with a lift?'

I hesitated, stunned.

'You need this,' Denny insisted. 'We want to give it. We love you both, and we want you to have it.'

I wasn't being polite. I was fighting a strong urge to say no. Swallowing my feelings, I smiled and replied, 'It's a beautiful idea. It's very generous of all of you to want to do this ... ' All the while I was thinking that once again we had been put in the position of being a burden, this time a financial one, and a charity case.

Kevin overheard us talking and was flabbergasted. 'You guys can't do this!'

'Actually, we've already done it!' Charlie Buchta chortled. 'We've even talked to your family, and they're chipping in too. We're not asking, Kev, we're telling you!'

Later I told Kevin, 'I don't know if we should accept this van. Didn't you hear them joking about us not having any more excuses for missing all the activities? Hon, you just don't have the strength for that. There are too many strings attached.'

'I'm sorry, Anne, I don't agree,' Kevin said. 'This gift is for our use, to make life a bit easier. Hon, it's given in love, not to make us do more than we'd want or be able to do. Why don't you want to accept it?'

His words stung, and they made me think. Was I overreacting? Maybe my disabled husband wasn't the one in our family with the real problem. After all, Kevin wasn't embarrassed at the thought of accepting such a gift. I was the one who was embarrassed. To me, that van was a symbol of our need and dependence. Was I simply feeling sorry for us? For myself?

'Oh, God,' I prayed that night, 'I've been so confused over this gift. Kevin's friends and family are giving it to us because they love him. Forgive me for not seeing that. Forgive my pride and self-pity. Help me to accept this gift with grace, as Kevin has.'

They presented the van to us in February 1989, along with a bouquet of roses for me and a beautiful lap quilt made for Kevin by Kathy Fina, the wife of one of his friends. It was purple and white, which were the college colours, and it had the college symbols on it.

That van has changed our lives, and it has shown me again and again just how much I need to learn to accept help gracefully. It used to take me at least twenty minutes to wrestle Kevin and his wheelchair into the car. Now I simply wheel the chair on to the lift, secure it, press a remote control button to raise it, and away we go. It takes all of three minutes!

Now, thanks to our van, we never miss a Sunday at church. We never miss a doctor's appointment. We go out for pizza every Friday night with friends. And as I write this, we're planning to drive up to West Point next week for a football game.

FRANKIE

by Victor Wheeler

I didn't like his looks and hated doing business with him, but I needed the money.

He was the first customer to come through the door of my new timber yard. The moment he crossed the threshold, his strangely twisted, scarred face and fixed blue-eyed stare repelled me.

He was in his late twenties, slight of build, and he held his head low. He spoke in monosyllables throughout the transaction. I wanted his patronage but there was something about his ill-at-ease manner that aroused my suspicion: was he honest? Was he heavily in debt?

In checking his credit rating, I found that Frank Dandridge was a cement finisher and concrete contractor. There was no doubt about his qualifications; he had served his apprenticeship under one of the city's most highly respected general contractors. Nor was his financial reliability subject to question. Married, he had one child.

Yet, underneath it all, I didn't like his looks and hated to do business with him, much as I needed the money. My attitude distressed me so much that I prayed about it. I simply would have to overcome my human feelings by asking God to help me with this relationship.

The frequency of Frank's trips to the lumber yard increased. Invariably, he sought me out to serve him personally, but I could not look him straight in the face for fear of revealing my feelings towards him. It wasn't only his disfigured appearance, there was something furtive about the way he followed me around the warehouse. Sometimes I had the feeling that he was watching me; other times I could have sworn he wanted to talk to me on a personal basis but was hesitant to do so.

Weeks followed weeks and a gradual change in Frank began to take place. His conversation was more natural; he seemed less tense. Yet still I had my original feelings of aversion and could not completely dispel my suspicions.

Then one morning Frank Dandridge came in to make a purchase. When his order was completed and put into his red pick-up truck, he scanned his load with more than usual thoroughness, suddenly turned on his heels and headed back into the office!

Naturally, I guessed something was wrong, and his abrupt manner seemed to confirm my fears. As I followed him into the office, it occurred to me that the common brick I had in stock was not of the best colour and hardness, and that a few of the bags of cement were packed very hard, though it was all fresh merchandise. I bristled, ready to defend the quality of my merchandise.

Neither of us spoke for a long minute, as my customer stared at me. A trace of a smile played on his lips, as at last he said, 'You don't know who I am, do you?'

'Well,' I haltingly replied, 'I know you are Frank Dandridge, a cement contractor, and a good customer. Other than that, I'm afraid I don't know much about you.'

There was another uncomfortable pause.

'I'm Frankie. Does that mean anything to you?' The contractor stood expectant.

Frankie? I sifted through my memories but could find no answer. My consternation apparent, young Dandridge asked, 'Do you remember a Mrs Standish who once worked for you as a bookkeeper?'

'I do, indeed. That was years ago.'

'And do you remember her son, who accidentally shot himself in the face while hunting?'

Of course, I remembered the little boy: an uncomplaining, courageous and, yes, handsome child – about eight years old. His father was dead and his mother had remarried.

'Well, then,' Dandridge continued, 'you must remember how you used to visit the boy after the accident and bring him toys and ice cream and draw funny animal pictures to make him laugh?'

My unattractive customer faced me motionless as sculptured granite. 'That was eighteen years ago, but I've never forgotten,' he said.

A prickly sensation travelled up and down my spine. That small boy, bravely returning to school, stoically enduring the taunting of his thoughtless classmates about his artificial eye and scarred face, had not only stirred my sympathy but my admiration. I had often wondered what had become of the boy.

Frank Dandridge was obviously that boy. All manner of feelings swam around inside me.

'But, Frankie,' I protested, 'why didn't you tell me who you were that first day?'

'Well, from the moment I read the advertisement in the paper announcing the opening of your new business, I decided to be your first customer.'

'I wanted to say "thank you" in this way for the help you gave me so long ago. I started to tell you who I was – I realized you wouldn't know the name Dandridge – but I thought you'd recognize me.'

I felt ashamed. All the time I had been trying so hard to find the good in this man, to overcome my feelings of aversion, to see behind his unattractiveness, it had been his very goodness that had brought him into my lumber yard.

Suddenly from deep inside me came the words I had thought of the day I first met Frank Dandridge: Look on the heart. I looked at him now and for the first time I did not see scars. I saw his kindness, his desire to be friendly, and I recognized a brighter radiance in his personality.

POINT OF VIEW

by Linda Neukrug

Can't you see things from my point of view?

The morning had been a disaster. My tooth was throbbing, and I'd been in an argument with a friend. Her words still stung: 'The trouble with you is that you won't put yourself in my place. Can't you see things from my point of view?' I shook my head stubbornly – and felt the ache in my tooth.

I'd thought I could hold out till my dentist came back from holiday, but the pain was excruciating. I started calling all the dentists in the phone book, but no one could see me immediately. Finally I got lucky.

'If you come by right now,' the receptionist said, 'the dentist will fit you in.'

I grabbed my purse and car keys, but as I drove I became sceptical. What kind of dentist would be so eager to treat someone at such short notice? Why wasn't he as busy as the others?

In the dentist's office, the assistant noticed my white-knuckled grip on the dental chair and placed her warm hand over my ice-cold one. When I confided my fears, she laughed. 'He's very good,' she said. 'You know why? Because he really tries to see things from the patient's point of view.'

There it was, that phrase again. What did she mean?

'Relax,' the assistant said, 'enjoy the artwork.'

Puzzled, I looked around at the bare walls. Then the chair went back. Suddenly I smiled. There was a beautiful travel poster, right where I could enjoy it: on the ceiling.

NEWSNIGHT

by Manuel Almada

He knows his clients only by voice.

Every day at 6 p.m. Raymond Flagg picks up the newspaper and wheels himself over to the telephone.

'Hello, Mrs Flower,' he says, 'are you ready for today's report? Well, first, there's the death of Hal Thompson, aged seventy-three, of New Bedford. He was a lawyer. Did you know him? Oh, I'm so sorry.'

'There's a happy item about Mrs John Owens. She had a baby boy.'

And so it goes. Ray Flagg is a news broadcaster with a unique audience, and one of the most appreciative: one blind person at a time. Each evening until late, Flagg is busy telephoning his blind clients to read them items from the local newspaper, the *New Bedford Standard Times.*

He knows his clients only by voice: their ages range from fifty-eight to seventy-eight. There is no charge for Flagg's services. He feels that what he does is its own reward.

'This helps and cheers me as I hope it helps and cheers them, too. What would I do if I were all alone?'

There was a time when he was. When his wife died in March 1965, the world became an empty place for Raymond Flagg. Overnight, the modest first-floor apartment where the couple had lived for twenty-six years became a painfully lonely place.

Flagg, now sixty-five, had no alternative but to stay in the apartment. He is confined to a wheelchair: when he was a child, infantile paralysis crippled his body but not his spirit.

One day, something a friend said gave Flagg the idea that has helped fill the aching void left by his wife.

'Blind people like to know what is in the daily newspaper but have no one to read it to them,' the friend had remarked.

Ever since, Flagg has been reading the papers to his blind friends: bringing the world closer to them and to himself.

Flagg is self-sufficient. He cooks his own meals and does his own housekeeping. A tiny pension supplies his needs. He is most grateful for that independence. 'I don't need help. Thank God for that.'

The man who is grateful to God for not needing help from others is equally grateful for the privilege of being able to help others.

MAN'S BEST FRIEND

by Carter Allen

As fast as we dug, the driving snow relentlessly filled in the gaps.

Not long after New Year's Day in 1996, my girlfriend Dawn and I were out late one night. It was snowing heavily when we got into my car, and we decided to go only as far as my mother's house, about ten miles away. I drove slowly, the headlights of my car boring white tunnels in the swirling flakes.

At about 1.30 a.m., half an hour after we had set out, we turned on to Mum's road, which is in a rural area near the northern town of Walker. There were only a couple of dwellings on the two-mile stretch leading to her house, and Mum knew all the comings and goings in this quiet area.

By now the storm had become a raging blizzard. The windshield wipers groaned, protesting at the mounting accumulation of snow. Ghostly drifts shrouded the road and I tried to keep the wheel steady. I shifted into low gear and Dawn gasped. 'Don't worry,' I assured her. 'We'll make it.'

No sooner had I spoken when we hit a hidden dip. The car lurched sideways and I struggled to regain control as we shot into a ditch. 'Hold on!' I shouted. The wheels spun futilely when I pressed the accelerator. We were stuck.

'What now?' Dawn whispered.

'We'll have to shovel our way out as best we can,' I said.

I reached on to the floor of the back seat. All I had was a brush. Dawn and I got out. Squinting against the stinging crystals, she wielded the brush and I scooped the white powder with my hands, trying desperately to free up space around the tyres. But as fast as we dug, the driving snow relentlessly filled in the gaps.

We looked at each other in desperation. The wind chill must have been way below zero, with the gale that was shrieking off the flat fields bordering the road. Our tennis shoes, jeans, sweaters and jackets were no match for the cold. We climbed back into the car and started the engine to keep warm. But in about fifteen minutes it died.

'Snow blocking the exhaust,' I sighed. We sat quietly for a moment, the howling wind stealing through every possible crack. Thick frost built up on the windows.

Think, I told myself. Mum's house was still a good two miles away, too far to walk in this terrible storm.

'Remember that house about a half-mile back?' I asked Dawn. She nodded. 'Maybe we can get help there.'

'I can't think of any other way out,' she said. 'Let's go. It's worth a try.'

Again we ventured into the blizzard, which had now become a white-out, and plodded through knee-deep drifts towards the house. After about ten yards, I looked back. I couldn't see Dawn. I couldn't see more than five feet.

'Dawn!' I called. 'Can you hear me?' Retracing my path, I found her. She looked dazed.

'Thought I was right behind you,' she said. She wasn't going to make it. I led her back to the car, settled her in and took off as fast as I could to the house.

At last I stomped on to the dark stoop and pounded on the door. After a while a porch light blinked on and a man pulled open the inner door. I saw him pull the screen door shut.

'I'm sorry to wake you,' I said, 'but my car is stuck in a ditch, and my girlfriend and I are stranded.'

'Can't help you,' the man said, his face set, and he started to push the door closed. I could see that he was old and frightened, but I tried again. 'Please, I just need to use your phone.'

'Don't have one,' he said, 'and my car doesn't work. Like I said, I can't help you.' He shut the door. The light went off.

What were we going to do? Tears froze on my face as I headed back to the car. My shoulders and back were tense from bracing against the driving snow. I trudged on, feeling weaker with every step. Stumbling on, I was dimly aware of something following me. But I was so exhausted, so agonizingly cold, it was all I could do to put one foot in front of the other. I didn't have the strength even to turn around and investigate. Too much effort, I thought sluggishly.

'God,' I said, 'only you can help us now.' Then, my head swimming in blackness, I pitched forward into a drift.

When I came to, a prickly, hairy form covered me like a blanket. What ... ? Some sort of huge black dog was lying on top of me. 'Good boy,' I whispered, rubbing my hands in the stiff fur under his neck. Is he wild? I wondered. No pet would be out in this weather. I looked into his eyes. He seemed somehow to want to help me, almost as if he knew why we had crossed paths.

I pressed my face into his thick fur and breathed the air warmed by his body. The dog stood up. What a magnificent animal, I thought. I had never seen a similar breed. Feeling new strength, I rose and headed for the car. I half expected the dog to continue on with me, but looking back I saw nothing; my dark rescuer had disappeared into the storm.

I found Dawn shivering. 'I didn't have any luck at the house,' I told her. 'But on the way back, something incredible happened.'

We huddled close in the back seat, and I began to describe my encounter with the mysterious black dog. 'What was he like?' Dawn asked. 'Was he beautiful?' I elaborated on the details, stretching out the story, as just the telling of it warmed me, and I could feel Dawn relax in my arms.

When morning light brightened our snow-covered windows, we heard the roar of a snow plough. Then someone rapped on the glass. The Good Samaritan driver took us to my mother's house. 'You were out all night in that awful storm?' Mum said. 'God must have been watching over you.'

I told her about the black dog who saved my life, and she looked doubtful. 'I know my road,' she said. 'There's no such dog around here.'

Then her eyes widened. 'But, you know, twice I've seen a black wolf wandering around that very spot—' She stopped. She knew it as well as I did. That dog, or wolf, or whatever it was, wasn't wandering. It had been sent.

BLOOMING LOVE

by Connie Kelton

Friends are like flowers.

Friends are like flowers and should be treated and cared for with the same loving tenderness you would give your garden. First, make your selections and lay the groundwork carefully. Plant the seeds firmly so they will not wash away in an unexpected storm. Cultivate with kindness and understanding. Water frequently with thoughtfulness and consideration. Weed out all jealousies and misunderstandings. Do not fence in; this is the kind of garden that grows better when left free and open. Follow these directions and watch a budding relationship blossom into a full bouquet of friendship.

2

MAKING SUCCESS OUT OF FAILURE

Obstacles are those frightening things you see when you take your eyes off the goal.

Hannah Moore

A PEARL OF GREAT VALUE

by Marcia Evans

Did the gift of the seed pearl come one day too late?

It was Thursday of my high school graduation week. Thirty of us seniors, fifteen boys and fifteen girls, had been summoned to a mysterious 'secret meeting' in the science room. Why us? We all wondered. Why, of all the soon-to-be-graduates, had this particular group been called together?

The science teacher, Mr York, met our puzzled glances with a smile. In his late thirties, prematurely bald, and his bow tie was much a signature as his horn-rimmed glasses. He proceeded to hand each of us a small white box tied with a pink or blue ribbon.

'During the past three years,' Mr York began, 'I've come to know you well. And I see something in each of you that makes me excited about your future. In your box you will find a brooch or a tie pin decorated with a seed pearl. That pearl stands for your potential – the things you have going for you. Boys and girls, the world is your oyster. Just as a seed placed inside an oyster can grow into a pearl of great value, so each of you has a seed of greatness within.'

As we untied the ribbons I bit my lip to hold back tears. How much Mr York's words would have meant, just one day earlier, to someone who'd never seen any greatness in herself! I opened the box and stared at the tiny pearl set in a silver brooch. Would have meant, but not now. The previous day, I'd learned I was pregnant.

The news spelled the end of a dream: my own and my mother's. As long as I could remember, Mother had set aside a few dollars each week from her job at the grocery store towards a college education for my older sister, Marianne, and me. Education, she would tell us, was the way to escape the life of the coal mines. The life that mottled my grandfather's face with indelible blue scarring, that drove men from their shift at Number 8 Mine into the many bars in our town, that turned strong young men into invalids.

I was three years old when my father was admitted to hospital. He was diagnosed with tuberculosis, developed from years of breathing coal dust, but at that time the disease was considered such a stigma I was told he was in the Army. Once a month Mother and Marianne and I would make the long drive from Coaldale to the sanatorium. I could never understand why all the 'soldiers' wore bathrobes.

Even after he was discharged five years later to a rehabilitation programme, Mother's wages often fed the family. Her dream that one day Marianne and I would change the pattern was one born out of hardship.

Marianne! Perhaps I would have lacked self-confidence anyway, but by comparison with her ... Beautiful and brilliant, top girl in her class, school orator, National Society student, drum majorette, Carnival Queen, Marianne seemed to be everything that I, with my braces and Coke-bottle glasses, could never hope to be. Five years younger, I was still in secondary school when Marianne fulfilled her part of Mother's dream by graduating from college. Now, instead of pride, I'd brought shame on the family: in our close-knit community, premarital sex was a scandal.

Dan and I were married two weeks after my graduation. We'd wanted this, but not until we'd finished college and started our careers. With a family to support, Dan dropped his own career plans and entered the Army. We had three children, and were transferred from base to base, moving ten times in seven years. Constantly uprooted, living nowhere long enough for me to do anything but settle in before packing up to move again, I would look at the little charm dangling at my wrist and wonder what 'greatness' Mr York had imagined he saw in me. Finally, I tucked my charm bracelet away in a drawer.

After ten years of being constantly on the move, Dan took a civilian job near our home town. It was great to be back in familiar surroundings, and great to be near our families, but of course the pearl had come back with me too. I hid it away in a drawer again, but it was not so easy to shut it out of my mind. Increasingly it chafed and prodded me. You have potential. Find it! Use it!

Now that our youngest child was in school, I thought, perhaps I could do volunteer work. I threw myself into children's theatre, a singing group, driving for Meals-on-Wheels. On top of all this, when the restlessness continued, I tried various jobs. I clerked at Montgomery Ward, managed a florist shop, taught aerobics, and even delivered singing telegrams.

I was busy, I was attempting to help others, I was adding to the family income, but still I was restless. I would open that drawer, look at the bracelet and think, 'Is any of this building on that little seed Mr York saw?'

At night, after the family were asleep, the old goal of college would come back and keep me awake, tossing and turning. But I was thirty-five years old! It had been seventeen years since I'd written an essay paper or taken an exam.

My mother must have guessed at my turmoil, because one afternoon as we talked on the telephone while I started supper, she said, 'Remember the money I saved to send you to college, Marcia? It's still there.'

I could only stare at the receiver in my hand. Seventeen years had not been enough to blunt Mother's dream. When Mr York had spoken of 'things going for you', I hadn't been able to think of a single one. But now that I looked about for them, they were everywhere! A mother's dream. A husband's encouragement.

It took me six more months to work up the courage, but in September 1985 I enrolled at my local University. Of course all my self-doubts enrolled with me. When my aptitude tests pointed to a career as a teacher, I was incredulous. Teachers were confident people like Mr York, not people like me. The tests were so definitive that I entered the teacher-training programme. By the end of the second term I was ready to quit. I was competing with bright young people half my age and feeding my family packaged meals in a dusty house. On the two-hour daily commute, I would look heavenwards and ask God whether a college degree could possibly be in His plan for me.

For self-doubters, quitting always seems the sensible thing. Our daughter Kerry would be entering college in September. Instead of straining the family budget I should have been earning money for her education.

One May afternoon in my freshman year, after a particularly stressful class session, I drove home in tears. 'God,' I prayed, 'If you really want me to stay in school, please find a way to show me.'

The following Saturday I ran into Mrs York at the dentist's office. I told her about the seed pearl and how it had goaded me back to school. 'But it's turning out to be too hard.'

'I know,' she sympathized. 'My husband didn't start college till his thirties either.'

I listened in amazement as she described struggles just like my own. Sitting on his courses, I'd assumed Mr York had been teaching for years and years; from his wife I learned that my graduating class had been his very first. I saw that chance meeting as the nudge I needed in order to stick out the next three years.

Sure enough, on graduating, I knew that I'd found the 'something' Mr York had seen. I took a job teaching English at a local school. Due to the years I'd spent away from school, I tried to bring the workaday world into the classroom. Newspapers were as much a part of my curriculum as the classics, factory visits and talks by local employers as important as Shakespeare.

Towards the end of my first year, the principal stunned me with the news that he was nominating me for a national award for excellence in first-year teaching. In the application, I was to tell how one of my own teachers had inspired me. Of course, I told the story of the seed pearl. Only as I described the way that charm had dogged and pestered me did I realize that it had functioned exactly as a seed in an oyster is supposed to: an irritant and a discomfort, never letting the oyster alone until it has built something larger out of that tiny beginning.

In September 1990, I was one of one hundred teachers to receive the first-year award. More importantly, Mr York was given a Teacher Tribute Award and honoured by *Newsweek* magazine. When the two of us met for a newspaper interview I learned how appropriate the timing was: Mr York would be retiring at the end of the year.

I learned something else that day: to the reporter, Mr York revealed that he, too, had seen himself as a loser. After getting poor grades all through high school, he'd drifted for a dozen years, going from job to job, unable to believe in the future because he didn't believe in himself. What had turned him around? 'Seeing other people's faith in me.'

Suddenly, I saw a science classroom and thirty high school seniors opening small white boxes. 'That's what we had in common, wasn't it?' I said as understanding dawned. 'The kids you gave the seed pearls to. You saw thirty young people who lacked self-confidence.'

'I saw thirty people', he said, 'with seeds of something great.'

THE RESCUE

by Ernest Poston

Cold sea water swirled around our knees, rushing higher.

My son Ray and I headed off just before dawn that morning to tend the nets. We were well out to sea and there was a good chop with a stiff, cool breeze. A big cold front was predicted, so I wanted to get the catch in before the weather got too rough.

I was glad it was a school holiday so that Ray, my seventeen-year-old, could be with me. But he sat quiet and withdrawn, squinting out at the sea. I could see he was still troubled over the blow-up we'd had the day before.

I let out a heavy sigh. Maybe it was the teenager in him, but he seemed to question everything I said. When he got that attitude, I was determined to break it. Yesterday, we'd got into another argument, this time about his school attendance. As usual it had been followed by silence between us.

I pushed my thoughts aside. We scudded along for fifteen minutes before pulling up to the first net. We worked all morning bringing in fish. By 11.00 a.m. the wind had freshened, and the chop had got worse.

'Things are getting too rough. Everyone else has gone in,' I said. 'Let's check one more net and head back.'

As we came up beside the next fishing net, the engine suddenly died. We began to float directly into the net. Getting a propeller tangled is every fisherman's nightmare. 'Start her up!' I shouted to Ray, who was closest to the controls. 'Hurry!'

He tried, but the engine refused. Looking around, I saw why. Cork from the net bobbed all around the motor. Too late. We were already snarled! Before either of us could react, the sea whirled us around, turning the stern directly into the onslaught of waves. They washed over the transom, filling the boat. Cold sea water swirled around our knees, rushing higher. I watched helplessly as our jug of drinking water floated over the side.

Since the boat was lined with plastic foam, it didn't sink, but the hull was almost completely submerged, and we were nearly waist-deep in icy water. I had no idea how long the boat could stay afloat; the force of the waves seemed strong enough to push her under completely. We had to lighten her, and fast. 'Throw the fish over!' I yelled.

'All of them?' Ray cried.

'All of them! Nets too.'

Everything was happening too fast. I tried to think what we'd need. 'Save the tarpaulin and the buckets,' I said. I grabbed a knife and went overboard to cut the net away from the propeller shaft. There was no way the immersed outboard would start again, but if I freed the boat from the weight of the net, it might help us stay afloat.

By the time I slid back into the boat, we had drifted towards open sea. I scrambled to drop anchor.

'Start bailing!' I shouted. We grabbed the buckets, but for every gallon we tossed out, the ocean tossed five back in. Cold, wet and exhausted we gave up. 'We might as well conserve our strength,' I said.

Ray and I leaned against a petrol can tied at the bow and pulled the tarpaulin over our heads to shield us from the constant pounding of the waves. 'If we aren't back by late afternoon, Steve will come looking for us,' I said, trying to sound confident. Steve is my brother and a commercial fisherman. He knew where I set my nets. Ray nodded and we fell silent. I guessed the temperature was around 40°F, but as we were drenched, it seemed a lot colder. I kept thinking about the cold front that would bring sub-zero temperatures and strong winds. God, I prayed silently, I'm turning this situation over to you.

The afternoon wore on as we knelt under the tarpaulin. When the wind and sea got worse, I peeled back our cover and looked around. We were no longer in the bay! The anchor had dragged. We were a half-mile out in open sea. Steve would have no idea where to find us now.

Ray stared back towards shore with a lost-hope look in his eyes. The waves were rising in seven-foot swells, towering over our nearly sunk little boat. It would be tough to spot us in daylight. And when darkness fell ...

Suddenly, I remembered the flares. I pushed through the water to the boat's console, only to find it empty. They'd floated overboard. I stared at Ray, his hair plastered on to his face, his eyes beseeching. I couldn't help but wonder if we were spending our last hours together. A wave came into the boat, spraying salt water into my eyes, making them sting, and blurring my vision.

'Ray,' I said, 'I need to be square with you. The way we're dragging out to sea, the situation could get real bad. If there's anything you need to get right with the Lord, I would go ahead and do it.'

He bowed his head. As I watched him, my heart was full and aching. I tried to remember how long it had been since I'd told him how much he meant to me. Why was it so hard to express tenderness and so easy to spout harsh words? We had let so much distance creep between us. I didn't want it to end this way.

'Ray?'

'Yeah, Dad?'

'I want you to know something. I love you, son.'

He searched my face. Some of that salt water had got in his eyes too. 'I love you too, Dad.'

It got dark early. I watched the light fade away along with the distant shoreline. The temperature dropped and the wind picked up. The waves started pounding right over the bow. Ray and I huddled under the tarpaulin, knocked backwards again and again like a couple of bowling pins. I found a piece of rope and tied it to each of us, then lashed the rope to the boat.

Around 10.00 p.m. Ray straightened up. 'What's that sound?'

We threw back the tarp. In the distance, a light was poking a hole in the darkness. A helicopter was beaming its searchlight across the water. We shouted and waved. The light kept coming, but then, about two hundred yards away, it turned and went in the opposite direction. Soon though, it returned. It came within fifty yards of us, but it turned again and then vanished. If only we'd had the flares.

We were too cold and weary to talk. I could no longer feel my toes in my boots. I heard Ray's teeth chattering. I thought about my wife, Janice, back home with our five other children. My hand went to the rope that tied my son to me. It felt strong against my fingers, a reminder that no matter what, the two of us were connected again. And it came to me: wasn't there a connection just as real between God and his children? Wasn't I tied to him no matter what happened? I can't explain it exactly, but right then I felt at peace.

The boat lurched violently. I tugged on the rope to let Ray know we were still together, that nothing could separate us. 'You all right, son?' I called.

He tugged back. 'Yes, sir,' he said. Then he asked, 'What about you, Dad? You okay?'

All night we tugged the rope and called to each other. Then, pushing back the tarpaulin, I looked out. A coating of ice rimmed the gunwales. Light was seeping into the sky. My watch read 6.15 a.m. The shore was a faint line in the distance.

'Did you hear something?' Ray asked suddenly.

I listened. A whirring sound was getting stronger. We saw a coast guard helicopter coming straight for us. Moments later it hovered over the boat, whipping up ocean spray, dangling a rescue basket.

'I don't know how you did it,' the pilot said when we were on board. 'With the wind-chill, the temperature last night was eighteen below. We didn't expect to find you alive.'

At the emergency room in the hospital we found that both of us had only minimal effects from hypothermia. Ray's temperature had dropped to ninety-seven, mine to ninety-five. We were treated and released.

I can't account for how we made it or how we were found. But I'll tell you what. There was a second rescue out there, one I'm just as thankful for. It was the rescue of love between a father and his son.

A PICTURE OF TRIUMPH

by Marie Gaskin

Taking heart from a little boy's tragedy.

When we found out we were expecting a baby, my husband Jeff and I imagined our child growing up in a perfect world, going off to school with a new lunch box, learning to swim, catching fish, riding a pony, skating on white sidewalks. How impossible those simple dreams would seem later on.

Our son was born on a Sunday morning in July, two and a half months early. He weighed 2 pounds and 12 ounces and he wasn't breathing. The nurse rushed him to neonatal intensive care.

The first time Jeff and I visited our son, I thought that as a registered nurse, I would be prepared. But when I saw him struggling desperately to survive, so fragile and tiny among all those wires and tubes, unable to breathe except with a ventilator, the blood drained from my face. As I gazed at my son, all my hopes seemed to collide with reality.

'We need to have hope,' Jeff said, back in my room. 'We can endure anything if we have hope.'

Hope. It seemed like the most elusive thing in the world, especially when the doctors weren't very hopeful. Besides his premature size, our son was very sick with toxoplasmosis, a rare disease that could cause blindness, deafness and brain damage – that is, if he survived at all.

When I visited our son, whom we named Brian, two days later, I noticed a stuffed dog in his crib – a gift from his nurse. Until now no one had brought him a gift, since no one expected him to live. I picked up the dog and gave it a squeeze. That small toy gave me a genuine breath of hope amidst all the grim predictions. I named it Sparky the Guard Dog.

The next day, however, Brian's condition worsened. 'Maybe you ought to hold him now,' a nurse said. A rocking chair was pulled near his ventilator and Brian was tucked into my arms. Then suddenly the cardiac alarm sounded. Brian's heart had failed. He was scooped from my lap as emergency measures exploded all around.

That evening, as a last-ditch transfusion dripped into Brian's veins, an eye specialist who'd been called in approached Jeff and myself in the waiting area. 'The news isn't good,' he told us. 'Brian is blind.'

Jeff and I stood there like two extinguished candles, our faces dark and silent. 'Are you sure?' Jeff finally asked.

'I'm afraid so,' the doctor said.

Late that night Jeff and I went home, but sleep would not come. In the silence of my bedroom I began to have the feeling I should pray differently. Surrender him to me, an inner voice urged.

Lying in bed, Jeff and I prayed. We relinquished the seemingly hopeless situation, and put Brian into God's hands. Then I fell asleep on Jeff's shoulder.

The next morning a call came from Brian's nurse. The transfusion had worked. Not only that, for the first time he was breathing without a ventilator. I hung up and twirled through the house, ecstatic.

Brian's condition gradually improved. Every day I went to the hospital and rocked him, singing every lullaby I knew, hoping he would come to know me by my voice. Jeff and I told each other that a blind child could still have a full life.

On a crisp October day I showed up at the hospital to take our son home. He was three months old. I was dressing him when the nurse handed me an envelope from Brian's doctors. Inside I found a list of homes – institutions and care facilities where I could send Brian to live. One of them was a home for the profoundly retarded.

I felt dazed. I shredded the list to pieces. Then I picked up my child and took him home. That night I found a permanent place for Sparky the Guard Dog in Brian's nursery.

That first year Brian was plagued by constant ear infections. I told myself this was why he didn't respond to noises as other children did. If I clapped my hands, he didn't turn around. Brian made only vibratory sounds, no 'da-da' or 'ma-ma'.

One bleak February day when Brian was eighteen months old, the doctors sedated him to perform a brain stem audiometry. Jeff and I stood in the dimly lit room, watching a green television monitor. I stood there, willing the wave forms on the screen to rise and fall, which would mean that Brian could hear. The lines were flat.

I wanted to scream that little babies cannot be born blind and deaf, that this could not be happening. Instead, I walked slowly to the car, clutching Brian to me, struggling to keep myself from shattering to pieces inside.

At home, I put Brian in his playpen and sank on to the sofa. Jeff had to return to work and I was alone. I sat there, gazing out the window as grey clouds scrolled down the sky, enveloping everything in semi-darkness.

I looked at Brian playing with Sparky. 'Oh, Brian, how am I going to communicate with you? How will I tell you that I love you, and make you understand what that means?'

During the next three days, I moved like a shadow through the house. I did not go out. I barely ate. I felt sorry for Brian, sorry for myself. I kept imagining what it must be like to live in Brian's world, where not even a trace of sound or light penetrated. What sort of life would he have?

On the fourth morning, still robed in gloom, I carried Brian into the kitchen and put him in his high chair. I thought of the night when he'd been close to death, how I had surrendered him to God. Where had all that brave hope gone?

Sunlight streamed through the bay window, shining on Brian's hair, weaving a little golden halo around his head. I stopped everything and looked at him. I was pierced suddenly with love, much love. And instantly a thought burned in me: Regardless of how severe his handicaps are, his life is a beautiful, shining gift, and he can have a future ... only if I break out of my prison of hopelessness and do everything in my power to help him.

I began to hope again. I shovelled oatmeal into Brian as fast as he could eat it, then dressed us both and headed for the shops. I marched into a bookstore and bought a copy of Helen Keller's autobiography.

As I read that book, I marvelled. Here was a woman who'd grown up deaf and blind like Brian, yet she contributed more to the world than most seeing and hearing people. I read about her struggle to learn, about how her teacher, Annie Sullivan, never gave up hope.

Soon after that I met Joyce Kirchin, a teacher at a school for the deaf. She took a special interest in Brian and agreed to take him into her programme even though she'd never taught a deaf-and-blind child. She also helped me learn sign language.

Armed with a repertoire of new words, I plopped Brian in his high chair one morning. I signed the word for juice on his cheek, curving my thumb and forefinger into the shape of the letter C and tracing the movement slowly across his skin. Then I put a cup of juice in his hands. After he took a sip, I took the cup away, and repeated the whole thing again. I did it over and over again.

I was about to give up for the day when Brian slowly lifted his hand to his cheek and formed the letter C next to his mouth. I gasped. 'Oh, Brian, you said juice!' I picked him up and danced around the kitchen. Juice! What a beautiful word!

I knew then that Brian could learn. Mama, Daddy, Brian, eat, sleep, walk, bath, fun – it was slow work, but he picked up word after word. I signed 'Daddy's home' in his hands and gave him a hug each time Jeff arrived in from work. One day Brian signed 'Daddy's home' as Jeff came through the door. How did he know we wondered? We figured out Brian had known by Jeff's scent as well as the particular vibration of his footsteps on the floor. Indeed, over the next four years we discovered that Brian was an intelligent child, with a zeal for experiencing the world.

When he was five, I accompanied his school on a field trip to a farm where the children were given pony rides. As Brian sat on the pony, he became animated. He signed 'horse' over and over again. I came away praying for a way he could ride again. A few days later a friend called. 'I just read about a riding programme for handicapped children, and Brian kept coming to my mind,' she said. 'I felt a nudge to call and tell you about it.'

'Thank you, God,' I whispered as I took down the information. As we neared the stables a week later, I took Brian's hands and signed, 'Brian ride horse today.' And when I lifted him into the saddle, he buried his face in the animal's neck, feeling and sniffing. As the horse plodded off, Brian broke into laughter. 'Horse fun!' he signed. 'Brian happy.'

At seven years old, Brian still rides every week. When I see him up in that saddle, I often recall those things we dreamed about for our child before he was born; Brian has done every one of them. You should have seen him the first time he caught a fish or went careering down the sidewalk on a pair of skates with me in full chase, or the first time he dived into the swimming pool and came up, spluttering. More than anything, I love his daring and his passion for living.

I've learned a lot from being Brian's mum. Most of all, I've discovered the enormous power of hope. Through the ups and downs of these seven years, I found there's nothing that suffocates potential and snuffs out the joy of life more than feeling boxed in by a hopeless situation. No matter what difficulty you struggle with, there's always a way to overcome it, transform it or find the best within it, if only you surrender it to God and don't give up.

Once, I felt convinced that I would never be able to communicate with my deaf-and-blind son or make him understand that I loved him. Well, today when I sign the words 'I love you' across his chest, his face lights with a smile and he reaches to hug me. If ever hope ceases to sing inside, remember that.

DON'T BE FRIGHTENED OF FAILURE

by Austin Pardue

How failure can be turned on its head.

Nowadays it seems that so much emphasis is placed on the importance of achieving great success in life that I sometimes wonder what becomes of all the people who often have to settle for less, people who know the meaning of that grim word failure. How do they stand it? How do they adjust? How do they come back from the deep discouragement that failure – or apparent failure – often brings?

I think, perhaps, that I have something to say to such people, because in my time I have had more than a nodding acquaintance with failure.

I started out in life as a resounding academic failure. In grammar school, where we were seated in order of our grades, I usually sat in the right rear corner seat – the lowest in a class of about forty or fifty pupils. And I discovered that if you sit in the lowest seat long enough, you begin to have a pretty poor opinion of your future possibilities.

I had to have extra teaching in the school holidays in order to get through grammar school, which must be some kind of a record for academic density. I never did graduate from high school. When World War I came along, I left school to enlist at the age of seventeen.

After the war, I decided I wanted to go to college and found that if you had been in the services, you could enter easily without a high school diploma. I arrived at college with a few pounds in my pocket, and got a job at a local train station, heaving trunks on and off trains early in the morning. I went out for football – and I sincerely tried to study.

One day, the president of the college called me in and said, 'I'm not sure you should be here; I'm going to give you an IQ test.' I took the test, and, apparently, it claimed to prove that I was about a middle-grade moron. The president called me in again and said, 'Pardue, you'll never get through college. You'll never be a minister. You just can't make it.'

The following September I tried again at college, and the same thing happened. Another IQ test. Another disaster. The president said, 'Pardue, what you should be is a farmer, or one who works with his hands. Anyway, you shouldn't be here.' So I was out for the second time.

I tried another small college called St Steven's, and the president there was cordial. 'We'll send for your credentials,' he said. 'I haven't any,' I answered. 'In that case,' he said, 'what makes you think you can come here?' 'I don't know,' I said. 'I believe that there is a plan for me and maybe your college is part of it.'

Well, they let me enter, but that didn't work out either. I could not make the grade. Before long I was asked to leave once more.

When I returned home I still felt that somehow my ordination into the priesthood could and would be achieved even though I was without money, academic credentials or powerful backers. My kindly rector had just about given up on me, but the curate at my parish church listened to my story.

He told me that he had gone through a somewhat similar experience, and he wrote on my behalf to the dean of Nashotah House, an Episcopal seminary that had a special preparatory department for men without college degrees.

I went there and eventually the dean asked me the most important question I had ever been asked: had I ever had a careful eye examination? I had not. He made an appointment with an optician who was amazed that I could study at all. My vision was very good, but my muscular focus almost nil; a condition later diagnosed as dyslexia. I was given a prism, and did endless exercises. A burden of inferiority was lifted: since primary school I had been convinced that I must be stupid.

So I kept going, mainly because my mother sincerely believed that 'with God all things are possible', and she somehow conveyed this belief to me. Finally I did learn to study and I eventually graduated from a theological seminary and became an Episcopal priest and bishop.

Now forgive me, as I'm not boasting, but today, despite not having a high school or college diploma, I have five honorary doctoral degrees, and have published ten books, which proves that God has a sense of humour.

I also think it proves something else. I think that very often what is hidden is a gift which the individual himself doesn't even suspect he has. No matter how low an opinion of yourself you may have, there are all kinds of gifts and each of us has some of them. In my case, I had a gift, but it was hidden behind my eye trouble.

I think that all of us should remember this when failure strikes. Just because you fail at one thing doesn't mean that you will fail at another. The word education comes from a Latin word meaning, 'to draw out', not necessarily to cram full of facts and information and dates, although these too can be important. Education really means to draw out the mysterious hidden qualities within an individual, to bring them forth 'into the light'.

The truth is, there are many things an IQ test can't tell you. It can't measure how much creative imagination, how much drive, or how much burning desire to do or be something a person may have. It can't determine how much willingness a person has to cooperate with other people, how much latent leadership he has, or how much perseverance he may possess. These are special gifts of God.

So seek your gift, and keep looking for it diligently. Don't let failure discourage or dishearten you. Sometimes the way is long, painful and hard, but by the grace of God, and with a belief in His guidance, it can be done.

EXPLODING HOPE

by Ethel Stewart

I bought her a large red balloon on a stick.

Several years ago I took my four-year-old daughter Carol Ann to an amusement park. Near the entrance I bought her a large red balloon on a stick. I cautioned her many times about holding it up off the ground, but there was so much to see that often she would forget, and finally it hit a sharp rock and exploded. The poor child, recovering from her momentary fright at the noise, burst into tears. My own eyes felt moist, but I stifled my tears with a not-too-consoling, 'I told you that would happen.' For a moment Carol Ann stared at the ground. Then she made a statement that has often given me pause for thought when disappointment comes along: 'Oh well, Mum,' she said, 'I still have the stick.'

FULL CIRCLE

by Ike Keay

A child's pain brings hope to others.

I work in a home for children, the only one of its kind in the country. It's a home for children whose parents are in prison. Many of these little ones have lived through cursings, beatings and broken bones. Some have even seen one parent murder the other. When they come to us, they don't know much about tenderness, about hugging, but know a lot about rejection and abuse, guilt and shame.

Here at Bethel Village we give them love, warmth and a caring family atmosphere. We don't have dormitories, we have homes. But even when the children leave us, there's something else I can give them, something I discovered many years ago.

My younger brother and I were born in Scotland to the son of a successful dairyman and to a sensitive young woman whose parents had emigrated to America. Father was robust and hard working; a good businessman and sportsman. My mother, Johanna, was gentle, delicate of health but strong of spirit, always ready to ease us through difficult times. I vaguely remember one of the most heartbreaking times for her. It was 1937, when I was five, and my brother was three.

We were waiting for Father to come home from work, when Mother took us gently into her arms to break the news: 'Dears, your father has been hurt in an accident. He'll never be coming home again. He's dead, and I think we must make a fresh start. So, I'm going to take you both to America to live with my parents in New Jersey.'

A few weeks later, we waved goodbye to Grandpa and Grandma, to the farm, and boarded a ship for America. Life there was rough as Mother's parents were not prosperous and were unprepared for the energies and antics of two young boys. Mother worked six days a week, while we stayed with our grandparents.

We had no money, but on Sundays, after church, Mother walked with us through a nearby cemetery; the most beautiful spot in our neighbourhood. We played games and sang and daydreamed together. While my brother and I snuggled in the curve of her arms, she read to us, including my favourite Bible stories.

Then, after just four years in America, tragedy struck again. Mother developed tuberculosis, a disease that had already wiped out much of her family. 'Please, ple-e-ase, let us stay with you, Mother!' I had begged over and over. 'Please don't send us away!'

Three days later, Mother's brother drove us all to a children's home, and we cried all the way. We wept even more bitterly as we saw our mother ride off, leaving us with strangers. Little did we realize that she was going into a sanatorium and was not expected to live.

The home was on a farm of 212 acres overlooking a river and a swamp. I saw the large dormitories – each housing twenty-one homeless kids – through a blur of tears. I was taken to my dorm in a state of bewilderment and shock. Oh, God, what is happening? Where is my mother? I was confused, frightened and terribly sad. My own little life was at an end, I thought. That terrible first day ended as darkness came and sleep mercifully ended my nightmare.

This brief escape came to an abrupt end as I heard a harsh voice barking, 'Hey, kid! Get out of that bed! It's time to get up.'

'What? Who?' I asked drowsily.

'Yeah, you, Buck-teeth,' yelled the gruff voice. 'It's six-fifteen; that's when we get up here.'

That was my introduction to the older guys. Because my buck-teeth stuck out like a beaver, I was called 'Beaver', or 'The Plough', for many of the years I lived at Glengary.

I was stopped by Mrs Patterson, the homeowner. She was a small, stern woman, over sixty-five, and so unlike my own mother. She had a rasping voice, 'Keay, did you see those boys smoking in the locker room?'

Mum had always taught us to be truthful, and so I naively admitted, 'Yes, ma'am.'

Later that evening the boys were waiting for me in the locker room. 'So you're a squealer, huh? We're gonna teach you a lesson!' One of them twisted my arms behind my back, and the other guys began punching me. My knees buckled from fright and I cried out in pain. They only laughed and beat me all the more.

'We'll show you what happens to squealers, Beaver,' growled one.

'Oh yes, I saw 'em smoking,' mimicked another in a high voice as he yanked my hair and pushed me against the wall.

When they had finished with me, they threw me on the floor. Once again I cried myself to sleep.

One morning I discovered I had wet my bed. The older boys found out and made great fun of me, forcing me to take an ice-cold shower.

For days and weeks and months, it seemed forever, it was the same – the older boys bullying the younger ones. I had never known such cruel treatment before, and I longed for Mother to come and rescue my brother and me.

'Stop that crying, you little sissy!' the boys would tell me. Then they'd beat me again, in order to make me tough, they said.

When I'd receive a letter from Mum, I'd feel loved again. She wrote to my brother and me faithfully twice a week, sometimes about the scenes from her window or about our father, whom we wanted to emulate because Mother described his attributes.

At Glengary every child had chores before and after school and on Saturday mornings. Either carpentry, maintenance, gardening or housekeeping. We grew our own food and did all the cleaning and repairs. It was hard, but it was good training. There were of course times to play, but I was always afraid to join in because I was seen as such a sissy.

One morning Mrs Patterson told my brother and me, 'You boys are going to the sanatorium to visit your mother.' What elation we felt! It had been such a long time since we'd seen her. After a long drive, full of expectation, our hearts sank when we were told at the sanatorium, 'Sorry boys, we can't let you go up to your mother's room, you have to be sixteen. Tuberculosis is highly infectious. You can stand beneath her window so she'll see you, though.'

We were not allowed to feel our mother's arms, but only to wave, and call up to her and see her gazing down at us from her third-floor window. Her smile was full of love, and it was the most love I had felt in a long while.

As the years went by and I grew older and stronger, I was not picked on so much. But I'll never forget the day when a gang of boys dragged me to the potato fields and demanded, 'Okay, Plough. We want a bag of potatoes, so start digging ... and dig 'em with yer teeth!'

I struggled to get away, but they tied my hands behind me and held me down, pressing my face in the dirt. There I was, surrounded but alone, humiliated and called all sorts of rotten names, digging up potatoes with my teeth.

In the years that followed, we saw Mother only occasionally. The wonderful mother whom I dearly loved was slowly, tragically, becoming a stranger to me.

Her letters kept coming regularly, except when she had more surgery. Then we wouldn't hear from her for a month or so. Finally a letter would come: 'My dear boys, my thoughts have been so much with you this day. I send all my love, and I pray for you each day.'

Sometimes when Mother wrote, it was almost as if she knew what was going on at Glengary. One time I decided to smoke on the sly because all the boys did it. We made our own cigarettes from corn silk rolled in toilet paper, and we lit them in a light socket with steel wool. Soon it became a regular thing because it got me 'in' with the big guys. Then one of Mother's letters arrived, saying, 'Your father was such a nice man. You know, he never smoked.' So, at the age of twelve, I vowed never to smoke either.

'Hey, Keay, wanna go out back for a smoke?' a couple of the guys asked.

'Naw,' I said, walking away.

'Hey, why not?" they asked.

'Oh. I dunno, I just don't want to.'

As I grew it became more and more obvious, I was becoming different. Instead of planning ways to run away from Glengary, I slowly began excelling as an athlete. My self-image gradually began to change. I began to do better in school. In fact, I ran for school offices and won. I applied for scholarships and got them. I didn't beat up the new little kids; instead, they came to me for protection. I didn't understand it, or even think about it much, but I was different.

Eventually it was the time of my graduation, time to take advantage of the scholarships I'd won and to go on to college. I couldn't do this, because although I was president of my high school class, I left two months early to take a good job to support Mother, who was going to be released from the sanatorium in six months. It was up to me to make a home for her.

Tuberculosis had claimed many of Mother's ribs; most of both shoulder blades, and half of both lungs. But Mother had held on to life, pain-racked and bedridden, so she could be with her two boys. After ten long years, we were together again.

Morning after morning, as I passed Mother's room, I would see her slowly, painfully, kneeling by her bed. Her thin hands clasped, her head bowed in prayer. I knew that even as her body had weakened over the years, her faith had grown deeper. One morning, when she heard my step in the hall, she invited me in. Only then did I discover that during all the time we were apart Mother had been closer to me I than I could have imagined.

'Ike,' she said, 'God has been good. I see a fine man standing before me, a son to be proud of. God heard my prayers.'

Mother told me how, in all the years that she could not be with us, she had prayed for us, constantly. 'I asked God to watch over you boys, to wrap you in His love. Ike, each day I pictured God's shield protecting you.'

Then I knew. Mother's prayers had reached across the miles, protecting us, shaping us. A mother I had seldom seen had the greatest influence on my life.

Not long after this, I, too, met the personal God my mother seemed to be able to talk to as she would a special friend. It was then that some of the missing puzzle pieces started to fit. I began to see how God could use the bad experiences of my youth to prepare me for a new direction.

Leaving my job, I went back to Glengary as a houseparent to boys like myself, so that I could show them and tell them that real love does exist. After three years I enrolled at college in order to be better equipped for this new calling. It was during this time that my mother passed away; we had been given six precious years together. Immediately following her funeral I learned the startling truth about my father: he had been discovered with a fourteen-year-old girl, an employee; and her father had called the police. They were on the way to arrest him when he took his shotgun and killed himself.

While I was still in college, I met my wife-to-be, Carolyn. After working for a number of years in various children's homes, we moved to Bethel Village where I became executive director, and we raised four children of our own.

Like the parents of the children at Bethel, my father had committed a crime. I can understand the disappointment and the shame these children feel. I know how they long for a home and for affection. And I know the suffering a child can endure in an institution. Surely this makes me more sensitive to these children of pain.

We do not have the children long at Bethel: by law, they can stay with us approximately eighteen months. However; we do have some leeway, because one or both parents may be in prison for longer than this; but eventually, each child must leave us.

As each youngster returns to his home, frequently one of neglect and abuse, though I am sad, I know that I can go on helping and trusting. For I can go to my room and pray. I can ask God to wrap that child in His love, and to give him the same, strong shield that protected my brother and me.

In times of great need, I believe there is a supernatural power that we can draw upon God's strength, the greatest force in all creation.

TAKING 'NO' FOR AN ANSWER

by Ben Patterson

Sometimes it's not the answer you want.

One of the bitterest pills I've ever had to swallow in my life was the failure of a magazine publishing business I tried to start some years ago. I struggled to make a go of it. I worked long hours, never really leaving the job. I made personal sacrifices and forced hardships on my family and friends.

Though I slipped deeper into debt and misery, I held on like a bulldog, believing that I must not give up, no matter what happened. When economic necessity finally forced me to abandon the venture, I felt guilty: maybe I had quit too soon, maybe there was one more thing I should have done – one, crucial thing that could have made the difference. For months I stewed about it.

Today, a long time later, I can look back and see a lot of the mistakes I made. Many of them had to do with the way I handled the business. But my biggest mistake was my attitude. I could not accept being denied something so important to me. I could not accept the possibility that the final answer to all my efforts was 'no'. Now I can see that I would have saved myself a lot of heartache, my family a lot of hardship, and some friends and relatives a considerable amount of financial investment if I had been able to accept that answer.

Over the years, I've discovered that 'no' is the answer to many propositions that the human mind can come up with. Not wishing to repeat past mistakes, I have learned how to accept that no without lingering regrets or crippling frustration.

Here's what I do:

1. I acknowledge that there is such a thing as 'the impossible'. A friend and former colleague had a saying I often remember. At first I merely thought it was amusing; now I see the wisdom in it. 'They said it couldn't be done,' my friend would tell me with a look of determination. Then he would wink and say, 'So I said the heck with it.' There are some things that cannot be done (at least by me). I can never become a concert pianist or a premier league footballer, no matter how hard I try. I don't fight the fact or resent it. I simply acknowledge it.

2. Remember that few things go according to plan. Just as the poet Robert Burns wrote, the 'best laid schemes o' mice and men' often do go astray. Life seldom turns out precisely the way we want it. It is filled with disappointments. Maybe that's not all bad. Columbus was determined to find a shortcut to Asia and failed. But if things had gone according to his plan, would he have discovered America?

3. Trust that things will work out for the best. The Bible says, 'We know that all that happens to us is working for our good if we love God and are fitting into His plans.' Like countless other believers, I have clung to that reassuring verse. Over and over it has proved itself true. Within six months of the collapse of my business, I was offered a job that was to become the most satisfying, the most worthwhile, the best job in my career. In many ways it changed my life. It showed me how God can work everything out for the good.

4. Get started on something else. The best way to accept a defeat is to go out and win a victory. It's not failing that makes a loser. It's failing to try something else when you lose. Like many others, I have often seen a disappointment prove to be a blessing in disguise. I admit it has taken some effort but I can now accept a good, firm 'no', and learn to almost like it.

HOPE BEYOND THE FLAMES

by Robert Wheeler

There wasn't time to wait for back-up, I had to act immediately.

Christmas night in 1988 was raw and blustery. I was pulling a 24-hour shift as a city firefighter. It didn't bother me to be working Christmas, because fires don't take holidays. Still, there's something slightly electric in the air when the alarm goes off on a day like Christmas Day. On a rescue call, you never know whose life you will step into, or who will step into yours.

It was nearly dawn. We'd spent most of the night battling a third-alarm fire at a timber yard. Now, as we were about to lift our forks for the first mouthful of a belated Christmas dinner, the fire station bells clanged again. Within seconds we were ready. I was assigned to drive the engine, so I enjoyed the luxury of being able to wear just a sweater and jeans instead of the usual 40 pounds of protective gear. We jumped in and sped off, the wailing siren splitting the silence of empty streets on a bank holiday.

We had a five-minute race to the blazing, abandoned block of flats. Jagged flames illuminated the night, and billowing clouds of grey smoke stood out in relief against the ink-black sky. Above the roar I heard screams from the rear of the building.

I sprinted around the back, while in front hoses were being uncoiled in a blur of split-second activity. As I looked up to see where the screams were coming from, I spotted a woman huddled on the fourth floor fire escape, silhouetted against a window. Smoke was pouring out through the shattered glass, and flames were licking at her as she cowered and screamed, 'I'm trapped! I'm burning! Help!'

There wasn't time to wait for back-up or the hoses. I had to act immediately. Only for an instant did I wonder what this woman was doing alone in a condemned slum on the morning after Christmas.

Scrambling up a nine-foot-high chain railing, I dropped down on the other side. There was no access to the fire escape; the drop ladder from the first floor landing had been torn off. I searched frantically for a path up to her. It would take too long for a ladder to be brought around. I had to find another way.

The drainpipe! It looked none too sturdy but it was my only hope. Wrapping my arms around the rickety length of pipe, I slowly shinned up the side of the building. I'm a large man, and I could feel the pipe straining under my weight. Above me, a rusty wall-clip holding the drain to the wall popped loose. I'll never make it, I thought. It would be a miracle if the drainpipe supported me for another fifteen feet until I could reach an open second-floor window. The pipe was too far from the fire escape for me to swing over. I had to make it to that window.

My view of the woman was obscured by smoke, but I could still hear her choking screams as I inched my way up. I heard the drainpipe groan and shift. A surge of adrenaline electrified my body as I scraped my boots against the brick for support. Somehow, I got a hand up on the window sill, gripped it for dear life, and hauled myself in.

Now I was sorry I wasn't wearing my gear. My eyes and lungs burned from the fire. I ran up two flights on the pitch-dark stairs to the fourth floor and dropped to my stomach: I crawled underneath the thick smoke, across a small room, to the fire escape. The woman, desperate to elude the flames, was hanging over the edge. I grasped her ankle and pulled. I couldn't budge her. She seemed frozen with terror. I pulled again and she screamed in pain.

'Come on,' I shouted, 'or we won't make it!' She pointed urgently at her other foot. Peering through the smoke, I could see that it was wedged tightly in the railing. Hot embers were falling on my back.

'Dear God,' I whispered, 'I need strength.' With one last yank, the woman's foot jerked free. Smoke rose from her clothing as I hoisted her over my shoulder and carried her down the fire escape. I jumped back inside the building through the first open window, and made a dash down the stairs and out the front door to an awaiting ambulance.

'Looks like she'll make it!' cried the paramedic as we climbed in. He slammed the door and we roared off.

At the hospital I sat in a hallway, catching my breath and sipping a cup of water. As my adrenaline subsided, I began to wonder more and more about the sad-looking woman who'd been all alone on Christmas. How had she got trapped in that tenement? How had her life brought her to this? Some strange and insistent urge deep inside me, an urge that I didn't understand, made me want to find out.

Her name was Sally, and the emergency-room doctors were treating second-degree burns on her face, arms and back when I found her. Sally smiled at me drowsily as a nurse examined me.

'You got hurt,' murmured Sally, looking away. 'I'm sorry.'

'It's you I'm worried about,' I said.

'I'll be fine. Always am,' she sighed, laughing softly and staring at the floor. There was something bittersweet and dispirited about that groggy laugh, something so sad and broken in the way this woman of thirty plus years looked away when she spoke, as if avoiding the world. Through the heavy stench of smoke that still clung to us both, I could smell the stale odour of liquor that lingered on her breath.

Later I checked on her by phone and was told she'd been admitted to the hospital. The next day I felt an urge to visit again. On the subway to the hospital I kept thinking about how our lives had converged in the flames of that burning building.

This was not the first time I had helped someone. It's a part of every firefighter's job to rescue people in danger. No, what this reminded me of was my own rescue. Like my father, I drank. I never thought of it as a problem – I was just doing what came naturally. Even when Dad died of cirrhosis at the age of fifty-four, I kept drinking. When I was happy, or sad, or just plain bored, I poured myself a drink. My boozing began in my teens and persisted through college. Eventually I dropped out of college to become a fireman. I started drinking after my shifts, staying out late and carousing. I figured a fireman had every excuse in the world to lift a glass.

One of my colleagues, Matt, knew the pattern I'd fallen into. He'd take me aside and say, 'Hey, Wheeler, ease up.' Matt kept working on me. 'If you ever want to talk about it, Bob,' he said one night, handing me a piece of paper with his phone number on it, 'just give me a call.'

Every payday people were waiting for me. Loan sharks, they're called. I was drinking up my salary before I got it. I'd lost my apartment, and that stale smell of booze followed me everywhere. It was no secret to anyone except myself that I was a drunk, a man on the way down. But I kept denying it. Even when home became a gloomy cubicle, I denied it. To make ends meet I got an extra job driving for a taxi service. Blindly rushing to meet a fare one night, I jumped on the accelerator trying to beat a light, and ended up crashing into another car. My mouth needed twenty stitches, though the couple I'd hit escaped with only a few scrapes.

'I'm sorry,' I mumbled, bleary-eyed and bloody. 'I'm so sorry.'

'Will you be okay?' they asked. They seemed more concerned about me than about their demolished car. As they walked off, I stood trembling I could have killed them, and they feel sorry for me! I'm pathetic, I thought.

In that instant, my life flashed before me: I'm twenty-nine, self-destructive, a menace to others, I drink too much and I'm going nowhere but down. I didn't know how to get help, but somehow I knew I had to. Before I understood what was happening, I was on the phone to my friend Matt. I remembered how he'd urged me to call him. Matt led me to others who'd fought the same battle I was fighting. Matt and his friends came to my rescue.

Now, six years later, I wanted to come to Sally's rescue too. I wanted to bring her the same message that had saved me.

'Hello, Sally.'

'Oh, it's you.' She seemed surprised.

'Thought I'd drop by with these,' I said, hanging up a new coat and hat I'd bought for her. 'I don't think your clothes survived the fire.'

'Thank you,' she answered with a wan smile. 'And thank you for ... you know, everything else. Maybe some day I can return the Christmas present.'

There had not been any presents for Sally that Christmas. She'd longed to go up north to visit her little boy, who was being raised by relatives. 'I miss him so much this time of year,' she said with that downcast look of hers. But her plans just didn't work out. On Christmas Eve she had started drinking with some friends. Then she drank more by herself. She had no place to go, no home. Somehow fate led her to the abandoned building, where she stumbled into a room with an old mattress and a candle. 'I didn't mean to start no fire,' she whispered guiltily. 'It just happened, you know, like so many other things. I'm so sorry. I could have got you killed.'

'Sometimes things happen for a reason,' I tried to reassure her. I told Sally my own story. It took her a while to accept that the two of us had much in common, but when she finally did, tears came to her eyes.

'I've been there, Sally. I don't know, what lies ahead on your path, but I want you to know that today, or tomorrow, or a year from now, you can change it.'

'I know,' she said quietly. 'I've tried before.'

I don't know if she tried again. After she was released from the hospital, I tried to keep track of her through a social worker, but eventually Sally faded one day at a time. Where she went I don't know, maybe back to the streets.

Yet I do know that I had been just as hopeless a case as Sally, and I had been rescued. Maybe my finding her on the fire escape that bitter night was an essential cog in the machinery of Sally's redemption. After all, had my own life not been saved, I would never have been in the position to climb that wall and save Sally's.

A RUSTY BOLT

by Daniel Schantz

'I'll fix it later,' I promised.

For the third time in a week, Jodie, one of my students, brushed me off. Passing my office door, she gave a half-hearted wave and shuffled down the hall. Something was bothering her but I couldn't tell what. I assumed it would pass. The next day when she all but ignored me again, a boyhood memory came to mind.

I was riding my bicycle, gliding, carefree, down the street, following a local political campaign, and stopping occasionally to pick up fliers and sweets the candidate had tossed to the crowd. My fender rattled against the steering yoke. One small, rusty bolt was holding it on. My father had warned me about it, but I dismissed his advice. 'I'll fix it later,' I had promised.

I was miles from home; I turned back, taking a short cut, even though I had to cross a four-lane road that I wasn't supposed to go near. I waited for a break in the traffic, then stood up and threw my weight into the pedals. The heavy, old Monark groaned, shuddered and rattled. I saw the next wave of cars coming up fast on my right. I strained at the pedals, leaning forward frantically.

Just as I was about to make it across, the front fender broke loose and slid down over the tyre, jamming it like a doorstop under a door. The bike stood on its nose and I went flying over the handlebars.

My body slammed on to the rough pavement and slid for about six feet. The palms of my hands throbbed with pain and the skin on my stomach burned.

I rolled over to see the cars and trucks thundering towards me. Tyres squealed and skidded and I dragged myself to the edge of the road. For a long time I lay in the gravel. My palms were shredded, and my tummy was oozing blood, but the worst pain was to my conscience.

All these years later I remembered my father's words: 'Better fix that before it gets too bad to fix.' Small problems grow into big ones if they aren't attended to. Good relationships could unravel if conflicts aren't addressed.

So, the next time I saw my student Jodie, I asked her, 'Can you come over to my office?' We needed to talk.

3

OBSERVING VICTORY THROUGH LOSS

Death is not a full stop, merely a comma in the story of life.

Amos J. Farver

A CHANGE OF HEART

by Jeri Boley

His loss was a tragedy for the entire community.

We sat in an office near the County Court, hoping to finally close the most painful chapter of our lives. For three and a half years we had waited for the courts to bring our son's killer to justice.

Twenty-year-old Brian, our eldest, had been riding his motorcycle home from work on 14 September 1990, when a drunken driver ran him down. The driver, Ruben Gonzalez, was convicted of manslaughter, but his solicitor had raised several appeals, the last of which had just been rejected. Now we were to be in court in three weeks' time, when the judge would sentence Gonzalez at last.

'They'll bring Mr Gonzalez over from the jail to hear his sentence?' I wanted to know. It was important to me to face Brian's killer one last time.

Our solicitor glanced up from her papers and asked matter-of-factly, 'Didn't you know? Gonzalez was released. He's got a son who's really sick. Bad heart, I think.'

I knew about his son, but I didn't know Gonzalez had been freed.

'Jeri,' our solicitor interrupted, 'there is a chance the judge might delay Gonzalez's sentence or waive his entrance altogether because of his boy; he may only live six months. Please be prepared.'

'Prepared for what?' I snapped. 'The possibility of Brian's killer going unpunished?'

In the car, I sat in silent agony as my husband Charles drove us home. Every day since Brian's death I had fought a battle in my heart against a bitter thirst for vengeance. Yet I also believed that the man who had snuffed out my beautiful son's life should be punished. It might teach others a lesson about drinking and driving. I turned to Charles and sighed. 'All I want is a twenty-month prison term with time off for good behaviour.'

Of course I felt bad that his little boy – five years old and also named Bryan – was dying, but I had lost my own son. I wasn't given a chance to say goodbye. Brian had been killed instantly when Gonzalez's vehicle struck him head-on. The sheriff had convinced me not to look at the body. Not an hour had passed since that I didn't think about Brian's death. I wasn't sure what I'd do if my son's killer were allowed to go free.

Our legal adviser informed me that I would be permitted to read a statement in court. I thought about what I would say. I'd try to make the judge understand the pain of a mother who had lost a child, a pain that becomes as much a part of your life as that child had been once. Brian was my first-born. He was a loving and responsible young man. More than five hundred people had come to his memorial service at our church. His loss was a tragedy for the entire community. He had died for one reason: a man had made the decision to drink and drive. That man had to be punished.

As the days passed I continued to dwell on the approaching hearing. The night before the sentencing I lay restlessly in bed, trying to read. Finally, in despair, I threw my book aside and quietly prayed that I would get through the next day. I knew that somehow I had to let go. I also wanted justice, yet I needed the strength to accept whatever the judge decided.

The next day the courtroom was filled with our relatives and friends. Mr Gonzalez sat glumly at a table, a few family members in the row behind him. When it was time for me to read my statement, I was asked to come forward. My voice wavered, my hands trembled. At one point our solicitor leaned over and whispered, 'Would you like me to finish for you, Mrs Boley?'

'No, I can do it.'

He squeezed my shoulder and I went on. I glanced over at Mr Gonzalez. He sat stony-faced. Then I turned to him. 'Finally,' I said, 'I pray that God will be merciful and let your boy, Bryan, live. But if you lose him, you will know the devastation we have known losing our Brian.'

The courtroom was still as I returned to my seat. The defence lawyer rose and pleaded for mercy so the defendant could be with his sick son. I barely heard him. Then Judge Gilroy called Gonzalez forward and pronounced sentence. Twenty months in prison, to be served immediately.

I just sat there, feeling no relief, no sense of finality. Was it really over? Was this what my son's death boiled down to? The stark formality of the process stunned me; I waited to feel some release from the pain. The solicitor said we could go if we wished – they were only waiting for the guards to lead Mr Gonzalez away, but I couldn't move.

As I stared at Mr Gonzalez's back, an uncomfortable and unwanted thought came to me. I ought to tell him I forgive him. I didn't feel forgiving, and I'd never really considered forgiveness a part of the issue, but the idea persisted. Finally, I whispered my thought to Charles. He nodded.

I walked up to Mr Gonzalez and put my hand on his shoulder. He turned and looked up at me, surprised. 'I want you to know that I forgive you, and we'll be praying for your son.' Tears rushed to his eyes and he said, 'I am so sorry.'

Then I hurried back to Charles. I did not want to watch Gonzalez being taken away. It was over. We could go home now and try to get on with life, but that night was no different. The ache, the anger, it was all there, and I still wasn't free. God, didn't I say I forgave him?

Gonzalez had said he was sorry. I had wanted to hear those words for a long time. The image of his sick little boy filtered into my mind. How many times had I wished that I could have said goodbye to my Brian? Or held him one last time?

I said I'd forgiven, but had I? Was forgiveness just a word, or was it an act, the most difficult thing possible?

Could I show mercy when my heart was so hard?

My mind spun all the next day. As soon as I walked into the house after work I said to Charles, 'I know this sounds strange after all we've been through, but I feel very strongly that we should ask the court to let Mr Gonzalez be with his son.'

Relief flooded my husband's face and I knew he felt the same. He picked up the phone and dialled the judge's office. 'I hope it's not too late,' Charles said. The next day we were back in the courtroom. Ruben Gonzalez, in handcuffs and leg shackles, was called forward by Judge Gilroy and told that he would be allowed to spend his son's final days with him, after which he would complete a six-month prison term followed by probation and enrolment in an alcohol-abuse programme.

'From what I have learned of Brian Boley in the course of this trial,' the judge concluded, 'I think that he would be pleased with all of us.'

I felt a warmth rise within me. I had never been surer of any decision in my life. As the guards came up and released Ruben Gonzalez, I could feel the chains fall away from around my heart. Charles threw his arms around Ruben who was weeping. 'Thank you,' Ruben whispered as I embraced them both.

Ruben's sister approached, carrying a small boy whose face was buried in her shoulder. 'Bryan wants to thank you for giving him his daddy back, but he's too shy,' she said.

As I stroked the little boy's back I said a silent prayer of thanksgiving. And in my heart I was finally able to say to my own son, 'Goodbye, Brian.'

TO LOVE THE RAIN

by Aletha Lindstrom

'You can't hate spring rain! It brings the flowers.'

Jennie and I first met at night school. She had just lost her husband, and her daughter was no longer living at home. My only child, my son, was now in college and my husband had encouraged me to finish my degree. After Jennie and I had completed the required courses, we started teaching in the same school. Frequently we had lunch together.

For a time we were just casual friends, but one day, when I was telling Jennie about my problem fourth former, we discovered we were kindred spirits.

'He's a difficult little character,' I explained. 'I just can't seem to get through that tough exterior.'

Jennie looked thoughtful. 'Maybe you are seeing him with just your eyes.' She was silent for a moment and then added softly, 'It is only with the heart that one sees rightly.'

I stared at her. 'You're quoting that! It's from *The Little Prince*, Saint-Exupery's book for children. One of my favourites. You know it too?'

Jennie nodded. 'I love it. I've read it so often, I've practically memorized it.'

Now when I think of Jennie, I recall that book, because Jennie, more than anyone I know, possessed the gift of seeing with the heart.

From that moment, our friendship grew steadily. It wasn't that I didn't have an excellent relationship with my husband and son, but my mother had died shortly after my marriage, and I had neither sisters nor daughters. I realize, now, how I needed someone to share those little, seemingly inconsequential, things that add so much to life; things that must be shared to be fully appreciated.

At first it was children's books. I was delighted to find another adult who loved my favourites. Even as I write this, I recall how Jennie and I sat huddled in a coffee shop after school, a copy of *Winnie-the-Pooh* open between us. I smile as I remember the two of us, grown women, laughing until we cried over the antics of that lovable, silly bear.

One discovery led to another. We found we shared a passion for double-dip strawberry ice-cream cones, for poetry, especially Emily Dickinson and Robert Frost, and for comic strips. Often Jennie would phone me, 'Don't miss *Peanuts* tonight.'

And it was Jennie who helped me with my problem child. One day I was at my wit's end with him. 'What he needs is a good spanking!' I exploded.

'He's probably had plenty of those,' Jennie said. 'Maybe he just needs sincere praise for anything he does right, and a hug or two each day.' I followed this suggestion, and eventually, because of Jennie, I discovered a lovable little boy beneath that 'tough-guy' exterior.

She also taught me to love spring. Her joy over grass turning green, tiny buds appearing on trees, and crocuses poking through leftover snow, was contagious. One April day I said, 'I hate rain!'

And I'll never forget what she said: 'You can't hate spring rain! It brings the flowers.'

So I learned to love spring rain too, because it did bring flowers, violets, tulips and daffodils. Loveliest of all, I thought, were the pink irises that grew so beautifully in Jennie's garden.

'I've never seen such a pretty shade of pink,' I told her. 'And those ruffled petals – they remind me of a party dress I had when I was little.'

That was the day four years ago that she insisted upon getting a spade, digging up one of her two iris roots, and bringing it to my house. We planted them together, but I felt at the time that we hadn't dug deep enough into the earth. Every spring after that Jennie would call and ask, 'Is your iris in blossom yet?'

'No,' I'd reply. 'I told you we didn't plant it deep enough. You'd better come out and look at it.'

Then Jennie would drive to our farm from her house in town. After a cup of tea, we'd walk out and inspect the iris.

'Not deep enough?' I'd ask.

Jennie's reply was always the same: 'I'm sure it's deep enough. You've just got to have more faith.' I admit I didn't have faith. That was Jennie's department. She was big on faith. But still the iris didn't bloom.

Looking back, I count the many other gifts Jennie gave me. The love of walking for one thing. We spent hours walking together down country roads and along suburban sidewalks. During those times I discovered the inexpressible comfort of sharing my thoughts and feelings, trusting Jennie would understand – and agree with me.

She did, but with one exception. Eventually, of course, our discussions turned to God, the Bible and faith. I knew that Jennie was a devout Christian. Still, I had to ask the. question, 'Do you honestly believe all of God's promises, Jennie? Do you believe without any doubts?'

'Yes,' Jennie said simply, 'without any doubts.' I recall that she was quiet for a moment. Then her eyes met mine. 'And you?'

I looked away. Of course I believed in God. Some Power must have created the moon, the stars, the earth and everything on it. 'Yes,' I said, 'I believe.'

'Without any doubts?'

I felt trapped. How could I burden Jennie with my lack of faith? How could I tell her that I felt dying meant extinction, and that with it we lost all the simple, lovely things that mean so much – family, friends, books, flowers, even spring rain? But Jennie was waiting for my answer and I had to be truthful. 'Yes, Jennie,' I said at last. 'I believe – but with all kinds of doubts.' We didn't pursue it. Jennie wasn't the sort to force her beliefs on anyone. And I've always kept my doubts to myself, perhaps for fear of causing others to lose faith, a faith I longed to share.

Then one morning Jennie died. Suddenly, tragically. My first reaction was shock. And later disbelief. Even at the funeral I sat dry-eyed. How could that closed casket hold all that was Jennie – her faith, her understanding, her beautiful, generous spirit, and her sense of fun and love of everything good? Jennie who saw with her heart? Jennie who was so full of life and who had so much to give to the world? There had to be some mistake. Or else this was a monstrous, obscene joke. I couldn't accept it.

And so I'd answer the phone, hoping to hear Jennie's voice. I'd walk along a street, expecting to see Jennie coming towards me. I'd read a bit of poetry or laugh at a cartoon in a magazine, and I'd think, I must share this with Jennie. One afternoon I drove into town and automatically turned down her street. The garage and house doors were shut and the blinds were drawn – like a closed coffin. Suddenly it struck me with full force. Jennie was dead and buried in the dark earth. All the things that had been Jennie – even the bright moments we'd shared – were dead and buried with her.

A dark shadow moved over my life. The spring days seemed cold and empty. The part of me that had been my friendship for Jennie was an aching void. I resented the first robins; what right did they have to sing since Jennie couldn't hear them? The crocuses and daffodils – they only reminded me that Jennie, who had loved them so much, would never see them again. But then came a night with a soft warm rain. I awakened in the morning and for some reason, I don't know why, I pulled on a robe and stepped outside. The robins were singing and a rainbow painted the sky; below the rainbow, in my flower border; a pink iris bloomed. After four long years – I could scarcely believe it!

I crossed the rain-wet grass in my bare feet, knelt by the fragile blossom and touched it gently. I started to cry. A robin came and perched on the fence. He cocked his head and looked at me, comic and puzzled. Suddenly I was laughing and crying at the same time. Then – it was the strangest, and yet the most natural, thing in the world – I knew in my heart that Jennie was beside me, enjoying it all immensely.

And I seemed to hear her ask as plain as if she'd spoken aloud, 'Now do you believe?'

This time I answered, 'Oh, Jennie, yes, I believe – and without any doubts.'

REMEMBERING MICHAEL

by Frank Bianco

I was overwhelmed by my own grief, and had nothing to which I could cling.

Marie and I were leaving for freelance writing assignments that June morning. We said goodbye to our youngest son, Michael, who in two weeks would be leaving college. Generous, outgoing and always eager to help others, Michael brought sunshine to everyone around him. I looked at his handsome face and rumpled his curly brown hair. Every feature on that face was dear to me.

'Bye, Dad,' he said. 'Take good care of the camper.' I'd promised that as a graduation present he and a classmate could take it on a trip out west. I gave him a bear hug. 'So long, Mikey,' I said, using his childhood nickname. 'Take care of you.'

Marie and I reached our destination, and the next morning set off on foot to photograph the sunrise. When we returned, the spot where we'd left the camper was empty. The brakes had somehow failed and the camper had rolled down a steep abutment.

We were waiting glumly at an auto repair shop when a policeman walked in. 'I've been looking for you,' he said. 'Your family back in New York has been trying to reach you.'

Now what? Exasperated, I dialled home. Our 21-year-old son, Jimmy, picked up the phone on the first ring. 'Dad,' he said. Why did his voice sound so strange? 'Michael's been in an accident.'

'What kind of accident? Is he okay?'

'Michael ...' Jimmy's voice trembled, and then broke completely. 'He was driving not far from school and skidded on a curve. He hit a truck head-on. He's ... he's dead.'

The days that followed passed in an anguished blur. I tried to comfort Marie, to be strong for the rest of the family. But I was overwhelmed by my own grief. Marie had her faith to keep her going; so did the kids. I had nothing to which I could cling.

I'd been born and raised a Catholic, and had even once studied for the priesthood, but I had discarded the idea of God as too unsophisticated and irrelevant to apply to my own life. Now, blind-sided by this terrible loss, I turned in fury on the Creator my wife believed in. How could a merciful God – any God – exist when my vibrant young son was gone?

At Michael's funeral Mass I knelt next to Marie in the front pew, my son's coffin so close I could have touched it. The congregation, filled with friends and relatives, raised their voices in a hymn. 'You who dwell in the shelter of the Lord.'

I felt no shelter, only cold rage. In the days that followed, I numbly returned to my work, carried on my daily duties. And as I did so, I became more and more aware of a devastating dimension of my loss. I couldn't remember Michael.

It wasn't just his body that was gone. My memories of him had disappeared. As the months passed, there were moments when Marie and my other children suddenly brightened. 'Remember when Michael had all those hotels stacked up on Park Lane?' Jimmy asked once, as we played Monopoly, and the others laughed, obviously remembering Michael's facial expressions, gestures and voice.

No such memories were there to console me. Even staring at photographs of Michael, talking to his friends, or handling his possessions, resulted in an emotional zero. Not only was my son gone from my life, but all traces of him were gone from my mind as well. I was unable to shed a tear; my bitterness toward God deepened.

The first anniversary of Michael's death came and went, but time, supposedly the great healer, wasn't helping me at all. I still was suffering a strange and cruel sort of amnesia. At night I'd lie in bed trying to see Michael in my mind, hear his voice, re-experience and gain solace from the good times we'd had together. I wanted desperately to remember – just remember – Michael but, try as I might, there was nothing. It was as if my son had never existed. That July, Marie and I drove to the south coast for story assignments once again. I had begun to think that suicide would be the only way out of my isolation and despair.

I went through the motions of coping. When Marie and I stopped for coffee in a small roadside cafe, we chatted with the waitress. 'If you're looking for stories,' she said, 'why don't you drive up the road? There's a Trappist monastery there. The monks support themselves on the food they grow.'

'Sounds interesting,' Marie said.

'You go,' I said. 'I'll figure out something else to do.'

I knew about the Trappists from my days in the seminary. They were considered a spiritual elite, a silent order known for quiet contemplation. They were also known for the most beautiful singing this side of heaven. Marie's hand was on mine. 'Come on,' she said gently. 'Let's check this place out.'

Grudgingly, I drove for several miles down a winding country lane towards the Abbey. It was just after five o'clock when we passed through a wide wooden gate flanked by high white-stuccoed walls. I parked the car and looked up at the words on the stone arch above the gate. *Paz Intrantibus*, 'Peace to all who enter.' Yeah, right. A nice-sounding sentiment for saps who were taken in by that sort of thing. I tramped along behind Marie towards a quadrangle surrounded by unadorned, whitewashed buildings.

On the west side of the quadrangle stood a plain-looking structure whose facade was broken only by a series of narrow stained-glass windows. 'That must be the church,' Marie said, starting towards it. The last place I wanted to go was into a church. I started to tell Marie that I'd wait outside, but she was already over the threshold. Reluctantly, I followed.

The light was dim and the quiet so complete that it almost took my breath away. Something stirred deep inside me, an almost imperceptible trembling. What was I getting into? I followed Marie up the steps at the rear of the church and took a seat in the balcony.

We looked down into a sanctuary built from clay bricks handmade by the abbey's founders more than one hundred years ago.

The walls were painted white. The alter was a slab of unadorned grey stone with a simple wooden crucifix hanging beside it.

Below us were perhaps fifty monks in plain-woven robes, seated facing each other in rows of wooden choir stalls. There was no talk, no movement, only complete quiet. For the first time in months, perhaps even years, I felt a hush spreading slowly, deep inside me.

A rap sounded. The monks rose with barely a rustle. Another rap, a signal for the monks to begin.

A shiver went down my spine. As the light streamed in glowing rays across the floor, the voices of the monks swelled and rose as one, offering in majestic cadence words from the Psalms that had been repeated over the centuries. The words were sung carefully, slowly, reverently – and with unwavering conviction and profound intelligence.

Was I shaking? Was the chapel moving? A glowing illumination filled the air. I glanced at Marie. No, she didn't seem to be noticing anything unusual.

I was stunned by a realization that left no room for doubt. As the monks sang, giving voice to liturgies and prayers that had endured for generations, I knew for a fact that they were talking to someone, and someone was receiving them.

Then, it was as if a door had been flung open. For the first time since Michael died, memories of my beloved son flooded me. I saw his handsome face as clearly as if he were standing in front of me. I saw him smiling and in my mind I heard him speaking as clearly as he had before we left that last day.

For more than an hour, as the monks continued to pray and sing, my senses overflowed with my son's presence. I remembered. Scenes of the happy times we'd shared over the years replayed in my mind. I was filled with gratitude that I had known him, held him, and loved him.

The bells tolled the closing Angelus, and as they did, I heard the words inside me, emanating from a source beyond any earthly comprehension: I know how it feels. I lost a son myself. I wept, and felt a peace. Peace to all who enter.

HOPE HAS A FACE

by Kenneth Culver

It took a terrible toll on Chelsea's body, but not on her spirits.

This is a story about two little girls. I knew that the first, Chelsea Ward, was someone special the minute I saw her in 1985 in the paediatric wing of the hospital where I was a doctor. She was eight months old then. Her parents had brought her a long way for a bone marrow transplant, a procedure that would supply Chelsea with the infection-fighting cells her own body failed to produce.

Doug and Jan Ward had the strained faces parents of seriously ill children usually had, but Chelsea flashed me a dimpled smile, held out her arms, and I was hooked.

The bone marrow was to come from Jan. Before she could receive the transplant, Chelsea first had to undergo two difficult weeks of chemotherapy and radiation. This meant isolation in a sealed unit that the nurses, her parents and I could enter only when kitted out in steralized clothing that made us look like astronauts.

For Doug and Jan it also meant a stay of several months away from home, in a place they knew no one. I understood all too well what that was like, recalling how lonely my wife and I had been when we first moved to the area from another far off city. So we had the Wards over for dinner and introduced them to our neighbourhood.

Doug was a top freestyle skier. I wasn't much of an athlete, but I did cycle to work each day. Doug borrowed a bicycle, and together we pedalled across the countryside, reminiscing about the impossible dreams each of us had followed. Doug's to be a champion skier, mine to become a doctor.

For both of us, finances had been the problem. Doug's solution had been to work as a coal miner; he earned enough in half a year underground, he said, to spend the other half on the slopes. For me, the answer had been to get the best education I could. I told Doug that when I was growing up my family lived in a less affluent part of town. I was named after the kindly man who had given my parents a place to stay just before I was born.

Everything that had happened since seemed to have prepared me for the fight to save children like Chelsea. I'd received a scholarship to college. Another to medical school, and then the chance to work at an internationally known hospital. It had been a long, hard struggle.

Now I watched as chemotherapy and radiation took a terrible toll on Chelsea's body, but not on her spirits. When I approached her cot in my sterile garb, she stood up, white security blanket clutched tightly, eagerly greeting me with a babble of baby talk.

On the day of the transplant Jan Ward was given a general anaesthetic. Then another doctor and I collected more than a litre of her bone marrow, an operation that meant plunging a needle into her pelvis more than two hundred times. Waiting out the eight-hour processing period afterwards, I felt my faith mount as never before. I always prayed before a medical procedure, but as I prepared to enter Chelsea's sealed room with the life-giving substance, I was emboldened to pray aloud with Doug and Jan, thanking God for the gift of medicine.

Ten days later Chelsea died.

As I placed her tiny, lifeless form in Doug's arms, grief overwhelmed me. In that unit for critically ill children I'd often had to stand with sorrowing parents. But Chelsea, Chelsea ...

Before the Wards left for home, Doug and I spent a silent hour in my garage constructing the small casket that would carry Chelsea back home with them. At the funeral parlour we tucked her white blanket around her before closing the lid.

The drive and purpose I had felt was now gone. I still loved my patients and laboured to help them, but a sense of futility haunted me. The high expectations that had sustained me throughout medical school, the certainty that God was guiding me – all suddenly vanished.

'Why couldn't I save her?' I kept asking myself during sleepless nights. I felt lost.

Then a letter from Doug and Jan arrived. They enclosed an article from a Canadian paper speculating on the possibility that gene therapy might help children like Chelsea. Her disease was caused by the malfunction of the gene responsible for producing an enzyme called adenosine leaminase (ADA), which is critical for normal immune function. Already, the article continued, experiments were underway to identify and correct such faulty genes.

For the first time since Chelsea's death I felt that God might again be pointing the way – a way as steep and seemingly out of reach as the struggle for my medical degree. If conventional medicine was not the answer for children like Chelsea, what was? Should I uproot my wife and kids once more? Abandon a growing practice? Leave my patients to become a researcher in some isolated laboratory?

'If this really is your wish, God,' I implored, 'open the door.'

Not long afterwards a chance encounter in a corridor led to an invitation to work at the American National Institute of Health 'in some field of genetic research'. Despite my misgivings, I took the new job. The day I arrived the lab chief told me what my assignment was to be. 'We'd like you to work on ADA deficiency,' he said – the very genetic defect, out of the thousands under investigation, that had killed Chelsea!

Without this confirmation I doubt I could have stuck out the rigours of this totally new field. My income was down, the cost of living in the city area, up. To make ends meet I took a second job at a children's clinic, while working ten to twelve hours a day at NIH. Building on the work of my colleagues Dr R. Michael Blaese and Dr W. French Anderson, I went at my experiments like a man obsessed, as indeed I was, by that memory of a white blanket in a homemade coffin.

Then a second little girl entered the story: Ashi DeSilva, a two-year-old with ADA deficiency. In experiments, genes corrected in the laboratory had been successfully reintroduced into animals' bloodstreams. Late in 1988 I worked with samples of Ashi's blood, supplying the cells with the normal gene and watching them begin producing ADA. Was it time to try the new therapy in a human being?

The DeSilvas lived in Ohio. I travelled to a hospital in Cleveland, where Ashi initially went for weekly injections to boost her failing immune system. A solemn-faced child with enormous brown eyes and beautiful dark hair, Ashi was able to leave the DeSilvas' scrubbed and antiseptic home only for these hospital visits. The little girl didn't know what it was to go into a store or to play with other kids.

Ashi's parents clutched eagerly at the straw of hope held out to them. On 14 September, 1990, I bent over a cell culture in the lab. The culture contained blood cells extracted from Ashi ten days earlier, which had been supplied with the ADA gene here in the lab. These cells were to be reintroduced into Ashi's bloodstream. After decades of research, a human was about to receive genetically engineered cells; the media waited to flash the news around the world.

Ashi, just past her fourth birthday, waited in the intensive care unit on the tenth floor of the sprawling NIH complex. Earlier that morning, without a whimper, she had allowed me to insert an IV needle into a vein on her left hand. To her this momentous day was just another in the series of hospitalizations that had made up her short life.

Down in the lab the cells were ready. I stood up and returned to the rest of the team.

'Here goes,' I said as I headed to the ICU.

It looked so unremarkable, this product of so much effort: a plastic bag containing a yellowish fluid. As I re-entered Ashi's room upstairs, she glanced away briefly from the TV set, then turned her attention back to *Sesame Street*. While her parents stood beside the bed, I inserted a syringe into the IV tube leading to Ashi's hand, for a small, initial infusion to test for adverse reaction.

For you too, Chelsea, I thought, and pushed the plunger.

Ashi's pulse and blood pressure remained unchanged. A nurse attached the bag, and the first human gene therapy was underway. It was a therapy limited to a single genetic defect, and it did not offer a permanent cure even for that.

Ashi would have to return for periodic infusions until we learned how to deliver the normal gene directly to her body's immune cell-producing system, but it was a historic first step. We hope and pray some day to be able to correct genetic diseases like haemophilia and cystic fibrosis. We hope to develop genes programmed to attack non-genetic scourges like cancer and influenza. We hope.

Whenever Ashi showed me her report cards and reeled off the names of her friends on her return visits to NIH over the years, that hope took on a face: the face of a smiling, brown-eyed eight-year-old.

During those moments, I thought of Chelsea smiling too.

A STORY OF LIFE AND DEATH

by Jenny Wade

Tim felt he couldn't face anyone, not even his friends, not even when he was dying.

My friend Tim died in 1986, at the age of forty-four. I'd known him for six years, ever since I went to work for a large corporation involved in communications technology. I liked him instantly, and liked him even more as I got to know him. His faith, his honesty, and his devotion to his family – were the qualities that drew me to him. Tim's death changed the way I look at my life.

At the time I met Tim I was an ambitious 28-year-old woman who'd cracked the upper-management echelon in a highly competitive, traditionally male field. I worked hard. My career meant an awful lot to me. Because I was a woman, I always felt I had to work a little harder, a little longer to get the respect and success, I wanted. Tim helped put things in perspective for me.

I remember once we were pushing hard on a project on which Calvin, the vice-president of our division, let it be known that he expected us to work all through the weekend if need be. This didn't bother me. But one day, during a project conference, Tim spoke up, 'John, I know how important this thing is for the company, but I promised my daughter Jenny I'd help her out with a jumble sale on Saturday at our church. I can't go back on my word. We'll have to find time during the week to get caught up.'

Tim found time – coming in early, working through lunch – and the project was successfully completed on schedule. He always put in his share of overtime, though he never let it interfere with his family life. That's rare in the business world. So many executives' lives are consumed by the sometimes cut-throat realities of corporate life.

It was because of Tim that I began to think of who I was outside the job, and what I owed to others. When Tim told me that he would be going into the hospital for gall bladder surgery, I was not too worried. After all, this was 1983. Medical science could repair just about anything that might go wrong in the human body, right? Besides, Tim had always seemed in such fine health.

'The doctors tell me it's a pretty routine operation,' he assured me over lunch. 'But I'll be off my feet for a while, and I won't be coming back to work full time for at least eight weeks. Or so they tell me,' he added with a wink.

I knew I'd see Tim back within six weeks, and I promised I'd pray for him.

While Tim was in the hospital I realized how much I'd come to depend on his attitudes to help straighten out my own.

When I was having a problem, I'd usually take it to Tim. In the beginning we just talked about business, but gradually I trusted him enough to talk over more personal matters such as my marriage or my faith. We both had strong beliefs.

Sometimes we'd even pray together. In time I saw that a lot of people around the company felt they could turn to Tim. Then there were the horses: our company's headquarters was located outside the city, and Tim's large office looked out on a pasture that usually had some horses grazing in it, beautiful horses. Often Tim and I would pause for a minute or two just to admire those elegant creatures. On hot days they would find a shady place to stand, tails switching. On cooler days we'd watch them prance and play. When it was cold, the horses would gather close for warmth. Something about seeing the tranquillity of those horses in their pasture gave us a sense of serenity, a glimpse of God at ease in nature.

I was eager for Tim's return, and a little surprised that it took him a full two months to recover. I remember being startled to see how his salt-and-pepper hair seemed to have turned mostly salt.

'How are you?' I bubbled that first day, popping my head into his office.

'Fine, Jenny. Great.'

'Well, it's great to have you back!'

But some of that old sparkle in Tim's eye seemed tarnished. Oh well, I mused, surgery is always tough. He'll be okay.

Gradually, inexplicably, Tim got worse.

He lost weight. He barely had the energy to get to work in the morning. Some afternoons I'd peek into his office and Tim's eyes would be closed, his head hung in exhausted sleep. He seemed to age a decade in a matter of months.

Although Tim looked as if the world was wearing him down, he didn't talk like it. If I needed advice or help, he was there. I felt a little guilty asking, though. Why should he expend any of his precious energy on my problems? But he did.

A year passed. An important project required myself and Tim to fly overseas – the sort of trip that inflicts a nasty case of jet lag on even the hardiest traveller. The strain seemed to nearly kill Tim. He spent every spare minute collapsed on his bed in the hotel. When it came time to give another presentation, he'd pull himself together and perform brilliantly. But I was really getting worried.

Then not long after we got back, Tim told me his doctors wanted him to spend two weeks at the Mayo Clinic in Rochester. 'They just don't know what's wrong,' he sighed, his voice an exhausted whisper. 'I don't have the stamina to have fun with my kids any more, or to help around the house – I don't even get out of bed on weekends. I don't feel like working, I don't feel like anything. I feel like someone just took my life away.'

This wasn't the Tim I knew. I could still glimpse a trace of his boyish good looks, but what I saw in his ravaged features was a terrible uncertainty, the kind of fear and vulnerability one sees in a very sick child who doesn't understand why he is suffering. That morning in Tim's office we prayed together, and the next day he left for Mayo.

I'm not sure what the doctors told Tim – I know they put him through a battery of tests – but when he got back he seemed reluctant to talk about it, and he continued to miss a lot of work. More than ever. In fact, I was the one who was travelling almost constantly. Between my hectic schedule and Tim's sick days, we barely got a chance to speak. I wanted to tell him about a job offer that I thought I was going to accept. It was a big career move and I wanted his counsel. But every time I stopped by his office for a chat, all I would see was his neat desk and his empty chair.

Sometimes I would stand at the window gazing at the horses in the meadow. They seemed so content, yet I was so disturbed. I all but wondered out loud to God why innocent humans had to suffer, why Tim was sick. Over and over again I'd ask Him to help my friend get better.

I accepted the new job, and when the day came for me to leave, I again went to Tim's office, and again he was not there. I taped a note to the back of his chair where he was sure to see it. I was sure I'd see him again.

Not long after I had settled in my new job, I got a call from a friend at my old company.

'Jenny,' she said, 'I have some very bad news. Tim has AIDS. He received contaminated blood during his operation. That's why he never got better.'

On the outside I was silent, controlled. I didn't know what to say. But inside I was screaming, No! No! No!

'He came in on Sunday, when no one was here, and cleaned out his office. He didn't say goodbye to anyone. People have tried calling him. He just won't talk.'

I thanked her and hung up the phone. I wanted to throw it through a wall, but instead I replaced the receiver gingerly in its cradle. It's just not fair, I thought. I'd heard all about AIDS, a fatal illness, caused by a virus that renders the human body defenceless against many diseases.

I decided I shouldn't call Tim. But what could I do for him? I couldn't force him to talk if he didn't want to. So I wrote him a letter instead. I knew that AIDS leaves the victim terribly debilitated. Maybe Tim was too weak to lift up his Bible and read. Along with my letter I included about fifty Bible verses that I'd copied on individual index cards, verses that had to do with hope and faith, suffering and healing, living and dying. Months went by. I didn't hear from Tim. Not a call, not a note, not a word through a family member. I know now that Tim felt he couldn't face anyone, not even his friends, not even when he was dying. That's one of the most tragic things about AIDS: the stigma, the same irrational feelings that block out compassion, the same fear that in years past made 'cancer' a dirty word ... Tim must have felt ashamed, deeply ashamed and afraid of the judgement that even his friends might pass on him.

Early in the winter of '86 Tim died. The funeral was a strictly private family affair, and no mention of the cause of death was cited there or in Tim's obituary, which simply stated that he had died after a 'long illness'. What the obituary left out was that Tim had died alone and humiliated. I didn't think it was right that my friend – or anyone – should have to die like that.

I was in my office when I first heard the sad news. I stared out my window, thinking, Oh, Tim had you turned to us, we would have listened, and we would have been there for you just as you were there for us. We wouldn't have blamed you for having the disease; we would have blamed the virus. Only God can judge.

Outside my new office window there was no peaceful pasture. There were no gentle, nuzzling horses. Instead, there were only tall buildings with glass, and quicksilver elevators, and people like me – ambitious, shooting to the top just as fast as we could because we thought that was what was going to make the vital difference in our lives. I began to cry – not for Tim but for myself.

I felt emptiness, a sense that my 'getting ahead' was only for me. I had been demanding to know why God had allowed such a horrible thing to happen to my friend. I hadn't received an answer. But sometimes we learn more that way. It wasn't necessary for me to know why God works in the world the way He does. I needed only to know what God wanted of me. Maybe there was nothing I could have done for Tim, but maybe there was something I could do about AIDS.

That day I called a list of organizations dedicated to helping people with AIDS, and asked how I could help. I learned there was a lot of work that needed to be done by volunteers like me.

Today, years later, I still work in my field, but only as a part-time consultant. I earn enough to take care of the essentials. I spend the rest of my time taking care of people with AIDS and talking to people who need to know more about AIDS. I give several presentations a week to corporations about AIDS in the workplace and about the nature of the disease in general. I speak to church groups who want to know how they can help. I explain that the disease is not casually or easily transmitted, and that our biggest enemy in the fight against AIDS is fear and ignorance, and our greatest need is compassion. For the first time in a long time I feel as if I am doing something Tim's way – not just for myself but for other people, and for God.

I still think about Tim. I think a lot about the horses we used to watch in the meadow. I remember how they pranced on nice days, lazed in the shade on hot ones. But mostly I remember how on cold, hard days they came together for warmth. That must be the way God intended it for us humans too, I think.

THE MIDNIGHT BELL

by Judy Armstrong

'Darling, I think we should stay up until midnight and hear the church bells ring.'

Mrs Webb was blind and frail and her health had been in decline for many months. She and her husband lived in the shadow of the local parish church.

On New Year's Eve she went to bed early as usual while Mr Webb watched television. Then, unexpectedly at 10.30 p.m., she came into the living room and announced: 'Darling, I think we should stay up until midnight and hear the church bells ring.'

In all the years they had lived in the town, Mr Webb could not remember hearing church bells at midnight on New Year's Eve. As far as he could recall, the local Parish church had not rung its bell in over seventeen years. Nevertheless, Mr Webb replied: 'Of course, dear. Come and sit beside me. We'll see the new year in together.'

So they sat and talked, waiting. Midnight came and with it the unmistakable sound of a church bell.

'There it is,' Mrs Webb said, and indeed the bell high in the steeple was ringing.

That was to be the last night that this old married couple were to spend together, for in the morning Mrs Webb was found to have died peacefully in her sleep.

Mr Webb did not know that the bell in the local parish church had been fixed only recently. Nor was he aware that a youth group was spending the night in the church, or that on the spur of the moment the young people would decide to ring the bell to bring in the new year. His wife knew none of these things either, but she knew the bell would toll.

THE GRANT OF TIME

by Ruth Boellstorff

'There's just no possibility that a man in this condition can continue living,' his physicians said.

One October afternoon nearly thirty-four years ago, I was quilting with other ladies in the basement of our small church. My husband Charles and two of our sons were home working on the farm. Suddenly the pastor called down the steps, 'Ruth, Charlie's had an accident. You're needed at home immediately!'

I snatched my scissors and thimble and raced to the car. My hands shook on the wheel as I drove the seven miles home as fast as I dared. Roaring up our driveway I saw the ambulance in the yard, and my heart froze. I jumped out of the car to see medics lifting my husband on to a stretcher. The terrible stench of burned flesh hung in the air.

My sons, their faces white, were nearly hysterical. They told what happened. They had been repairing farm machinery in the shop when a pan of petrol, which was used to clean parts, caught fire. I hovered over Charlie on the stretcher as he whispered, 'It's bad, honey ... it's bad ... I love you ...' Then he slipped into unconsciousness.

'Take care of things here, boys!' I called to my sons. 'I'll go with Dad,' and I scrambled into the ambulance.

At the hospital a doctor stepped into the waiting room. 'I'm sorry, Mrs Boellstorff,' he said gravely, 'but we don't see how your husband can make it.'

I crumpled in despair, but then, getting hold of myself, I began praying. 'Oh Lord, keep him with us, please. We all need him so.'

Day after day Charlie hung on, surprising the doctors. He endured agonizing pain as the days turned to weeks, then months. Even so, the doctors held out no hope. 'There's just no possibility that a man in this condition, can continue living,' his physicians said.

Finally, Charlie was transferred to another hospital where a noted plastic surgeon, Dr Albert Black, began a series of excruciating skin grafts to cover vast areas on Charlie's lower body where the dermis had been totally destroyed. Week after week on Wednesday mornings Charlie was taken to surgery. And he grew weaker. Then, during the eleventh operation, his tired heart faltered and stopped. It took heroic measures to start it beating again. His doctor informed me that there could be no more grafts. The stubborn flame of life that had thus far sustained him was flickering too low.

For days, Charlie lay immobilized on a Stryker frame. At intervals the nurses and I would bolt a metal and canvas lid over him and flip the entire unit over. This was to preserve circulation and enable nurses to bathe and medicate the burned areas.

Time dragged by for Charlie in a blur of pain and drugs. Repeatedly I was warned to prepare for his death. I hovered near, helplessly trying to comfort, to encourage, and I prayed constantly.

Winter passed. The trees outside the hospital windows were turning green, and still Charlie grew weaker. He had no appetite, and his big frame was wasting away behind the intense blue eyes and brave smile. There were times when, torn by fatigue and battered by doubt, I found myself in rebellion. Why didn't God answer my prayers? Didn't He care?

Things were not going well at home either. Our daughter had returned home from college to keep house for her brothers, but they found running the farm and managing the livestock an enormous task. Charlie's black Labrador, Cub, especially missed him. The dog moped and his brown eyes had lost their lustre.

One evening in early May I was trying not to think of all this as I sat by the Stryker frame. I had never before been able to penetrate the thick layers of pain and confusing fog of drugs to reach Charlie with an encouraging verse from the Bible. He simply seemed not to hear. But now his eyes fixed on mine as I whispered the twenty-third psalm. 'He lets me rest in fields of green grass, and leads me to quiet pools of fresh water ...'

The blue eyes never wavered. 'Go on,' he whispered when I paused. I stumbled a bit over the next phrases. It was so long ago I had learned them. Then memory flooded back. 'Even if I go through the deepest darkness, I will not be afraid Lord ...' Now he was saying it with me in husky bits and snatches. Together we finished: 'You fill my cup to the brim. I know that your goodness and love will be with me all my life; and your house will be my home as long as I live.' Tears were running down my face, and I could hardly see as I kissed him goodnight.

The next morning there was a strange new light in Charlie's eyes. He motioned me close to him. 'I prayed,' he whispered. 'I asked God for twenty more years of life.' He reached out a thin hand to mine. 'He spoke His promise,' he said, his voice strained with emotion. 'I know I heard Him speak.'

I nodded, not really taking him seriously. Many times the drugs had caused his mind to wander. When the nurse brought in Charlie's breakfast tray I was surprised by his new willingness to eat. When I commented on it, Charlie said, 'God promised to heal me, don't you remember? I'm going to get well. I need to eat!'

From that day he did begin to improve! The infection subsided. Grafts began to heal, and the areas between them sealed over. The doctors were amazed. Finally Charlie could be lifted from the Stryker frame and put into an ordinary hospital bed.

A week after that a physical therapist arrived with three strong aides. Carefully they lifted Charlie into a wheelchair. Since neither his hips nor his back could bend, he rode in a semi-reclining position. But he was out of bed, out of the room, and down the hall to the therapy department.

So began the battle to regain lost mobility. Therapists moved his frozen joints manually. They lifted him into whirlpool baths. They stood him post-like between parallel bars to regain his sense of balance. Painfully, he began to inch a few steps, holding to the bars. Then came a walker. At last he was released from the hospital. We could go home. Home, after ten months – home!

The doctor gave me final instructions about diet, medication, and exercise. Casually, he remarked, 'Don't expect this man to walk.'

'What do you mean?' I asked in disbelief.

'Oh, he'll be able to get around in the house, perhaps, with a walker or crutches, but don't expect much more. There has been too much damage.'

I was stunned. Somehow I managed to keep this dreadful knowledge to myself. But it was so good to be home.

Charlie's black Labrador went wild, dancing around him in circles. And though I missed the hospital equipment and found care of an invalid a frightening burden, life became pretty normal. Charlie's courage never wavered, and by degrees, he grew stronger. The day he made it to the bathroom alone, the entire family cheered. When he limped out into the late summer sunshine, I wept with happiness. One leg was to remain stiff for ever, but before winter Charlie was walking almost everywhere with a cane.

Spring found him pruning his orchard, planting new trees. He drove the combine at harvest, and he also bought a few cattle and fed them. He went fishing again, and roamed the fields with Cub at his side. Months turned into years. One by one the children left, and we were alone. Each day was a gift and a blessing. We had learned there are things we know without understanding.

Those years were rich and full. Then ominous signs appeared. An illness. An operation was needed. Another. A third. Radiation treatments. All to no avail.

On 13 May 1978 God called Charlie home. Once again I was crushed and I found myself looking ahead to a life of desolation. But several weeks later, while thumbing through my diary, the realization of what had happened came startlingly alive to me.

It was in May 1958 that my husband made his plea in the hospital for twenty more years of life and received God's promise. If ever I had doubted that God answers prayer, I could not have been given greater reassurance. For from the time of Charlie's prayer, he lived exactly twenty years.

THE WALL

by Duery Felton

This wall of more than 58,000 names has become a healing wall.

As the curator at the Vietnam Veterans Memorial in Washington DC, I help identify and catalogue the thousands of mementoes visitors have left at the wall. Some are remarkable, some mysterious; all have a story to tell.

An M16 rifle was left by a Vietnam veteran who was once given the assignment of salvaging combat gear from soldiers killed in action. As he removed the clip from one body he found himself staring into the sightless eyes of a friend.

Another veteran left an autographed baseball in honour of the many young men and women who never got to see the sporting greats of today.

A set of wedding rings was left for a soldier who had got married before going off to war. His best friend brought them to the memorial because it is 'where his spirit now resides'.

A watch bore a note from the donor explaining how his best friend Gary had prodded him into purchasing it at a shop during the war. Afterwards, Gary kept asking him, 'What time is it?' Now Gary will always have the same answer to his question.

Then there was the marine back from the gulf war who left his father's silver medal. His note read, 'To Dad, love your son.'

A bicycle mudguard was left in fond remembrance of a friend known for riding a bike without mudguards.

A Soviet toast cup was left with a birthday card inscribed, 'On what would have been your fortieth. Your loving family who misses you.'

For a long time I wondered about the two tins of sardines left at the wall. Then a veteran's letter explained: his friend had taken a carton of cigarettes from him and left the sardines. Later that day his friend was killed and now the donor had returned the much-cherished prize.

For millions of visitors, the memorial is a vivid reminder of birthdays never reached, goals never met, and promises never kept. So they bring their gifts to soothe their hurt and release their grief. In their outpouring of love, people of all races, cultures and faiths come together. This wall of more than 58,000 names has become a healing wall.

THE CHAIR THAT SANG

by Melissa Young

I finally realized that Grandma hadn't been stolen from me.

When I was a child, my favourite day of the week was laundry day. I used to help Grandma carry the overflowing clothes baskets down the wooden stairs to our basement. Then, while she sorted the colours and put loads in the washer, I played house in a huge cardboard box that had once contained our television.

When the first washer load was done, Grandma always sat me on top of the dryer. There I waited impatiently for the cold white machine to become nice and warm. As the last load of clothes spun in the dryer, Grandma scooped me on to her lap, and she and I rocked back and forth in the old green rocking chair. Grandma told me that the chair, which groaned and creaked under our weight, was singing.

To my young ears the chair seemed to send out perfect harmonies that meshed with Grandma's songs about little brown jugs and mares that ate oats. I never quite learned all the words to the songs, because I usually dozed off in her arms.

When the buzzing of the dryer eventually woke me, the songs were over and Grandma was gently nudging me off her lap so she could go on to her next project. All too soon our wonderful days in the basement were brought to a close. I went off to nursery school and Mum, who had got divorced soon after I was born, remarried. Mum, my new father, my two older sisters and I moved into a house across the other side of our town. However, I still got to spend most weekends at Grandma and Grandpa's house.

As I grew older, I began to see that there was something wrong with Grandma. She developed a tumour that doctors removed, then another that kept her in the hospital for much longer than the first one. When I visited her, she didn't seem to understand what I was saying.

Early one January morning Grandma died. Everyone told me she was better off. She was no longer in pain and she was with God. Eventually I adjusted to her being gone, but I could never reconcile myself to the fact that God had stolen her away from me. I felt deprived – He had Grandma and I did not. Every time I came across a letter she'd written or saw a picture of her, I burst into resentful tears.

Then one crisp winter morning five years later, all that changed. When my alarm clock first went off, I drowsily hit the snooze button, closed my eyes and pulled the blankets tight around my chin. As the warmth of the covers relaxed me, I drifted off ... and was back in the basement on laundry day, with warm arms around me.

There were the familiar piles of clothes, separated by colours, on the bare grey floor. I could hear the mechanical whir of the dryer, and a slow rocking motion started as Grandma pulled me closer. I looked up, and there was Grandma's kind, smiling face. I was a child again, nestling in that familiar lap, gently rocking back and forth on the chair that sang. I listened happily as Grandma accompanied it, tenderly crooning all my favourite melodies in the voice I had missed so dearly.

I pressed my head against her shoulder and closed my eyes, comforted by the presence I knew so well. Then a soft buzzing sounded from far away. When I opened my eyes, I was back in my bed groping to turn off the alarm. Suddenly, and with a feeling of great peace, I realized that God had just sent me back to the chair that sang to remind me that Grandma hadn't been stolen from me. In those magical minutes I had finally been able to understand that those we love will always be with us. I looked out of my window at the amber sunrise, and once again there was singing, but now it was in my own heart.

LESSONS FROM LOIS

by Carol Kuykendall

In a single day everything changed suddenly.

From the moment Lois and I met on a tennis court all those years ago, when our children were babies, I was drawn to her mixture of honesty and encouragement. 'Your backhand is better than your forehand,' she told me bluntly that first day, which kind of miffed me because I wasn't used to having friends tell me the truth. 'But you're okay,' she smiled. 'Let's play often.' We did, and soon our friendship grew beyond the tennis court.

When she was divorced, I was there. When my mother died, she was there. When she remarried, I brought the punch bowl and helped host her garden reception. When she found out why she couldn't get rid of her cough, she called me. I'll never forget that conversation.

'Got a minute?' she asked, when I answered the phone early one morning. She knew me better. I was always running late, but something in her voice made me know I had a minute.

'Sure,' I answered. 'What's up?'

'I have inoperable cancer in both lungs,' she announced, her voice faltering.

I closed my eyes and shook my head in disbelief. 'No, Lois,' I moaned. 'That doesn't make sense!'

Lois was forty-three years old. Her parents were healthy and in their seventies. She had never smoked, she checked ingredients on product labels and she jogged regularly.

'What does this mean?' I asked.

'I'll take a leave of absence from teaching and start chemotherapy soon,' she answered. 'I'll probably get real sick for a while ...'

'We'll pray, Lois,' I vowed in angry determination, 'for a miracle!'

'We need one. If the chemotherapy doesn't work, the doctor says I'm in serious trouble.' She stopped, and I knew she was crying.

'Oh, Lois ...' I shook my head again, aching for her, and not knowing what to say. When I hung up, I sank down on my bed and punched the pillow. How could this happen to someone so young, so active? So much like me? 'Please, Lord,' I prayed, 'give me the strength to walk beside Lois on this journey and don't let my own fears get in the way.'

In the beginning, Lois was determined to fight but she also confessed her own fears. 'I can't stand the thought of losing my hair,' she said sorrowfully one day as she looked in the mirror. 'What if I can't drive any more, or get too weak to walk, or have to stay in bed all day?'

I didn't have many good answers, but I got her a tennis hat, with 'Lois' Lid' embroidered on the brim, to cover her head should her hair start thinning, and I promised to rig up a giant catapult system to get her out of bed if she felt weak. Mostly I listened to her, not daring to tell her that the thought of her dying scared me too.

After several weeks of chemotherapy, her X-rays showed a forty-five per cent reduction of the tumours, and we rejoiced. She talked about going back to teaching. Her husband Don traded in her old car for one with better air-conditioning, so that she'd be more comfortable on warm days. Together Lois and Don planned a dream trip to Hawaii. But in a single day everything changed suddenly.

When I next stopped by, her fifteen-year-old daughter answered the door. 'Mum's having trouble breathing,' she said, 'and the doctor wants her to go to the hospital right away.' In minutes we were on our way. An X-ray showed a critical build up of fluid around her heart. 'We're going to have to do surgery immediately,' the doctor told her gently.

'I'll call Don.' Instinctively I reached for her hand as she lay on the bed, but she had a faraway look in her eyes as if she was focusing on something beyond me, beyond the doctor's words. Soon a nurse came and wheeled her to intensive care.

'This is not good,' the doctor told me quietly.

The surgery went well, but when I saw Lois again a couple of days later she was hooked up to a maze of tubes. I stood at the foot of her bed and gently squeezed her toes.

'I don't think we're going to lick this thing,' she told me with a half-smile. 'I've been thinking lots about how God turns fears into courage and gives us the courage to take one step at a time.'

A few days later Lois came home and turned a corner in her journey. Instead of fighting to live, she began preparing to die, determined to make the most of the time she had left. For a while she seemed to have more physical energy than before. She flew to California to visit her parents, and was doing so well that she insisted on going through with Don's and her plans to go to Hawaii.

'How do you like my new wig?' she asked with a giggle, as she packed a wad of dark curly hair into her suitcase. Equipped with all sorts of medication, Lois and Don took off. 'Having a great time,' the postcard said, 'glad you're not here.'

When she returned, Lois began sorting through boxes of family photographs and pasting them into albums. She asked me to help her type a detailed family history. She wrote loving letters of motherly advice to her son and daughter and explained how to make the family's traditional Christmas peanut brittle. With all that done, she asked me to come over and help her with one final detail.

'I'm planning my memorial service and I'd like you to do my eulogy,' she said simply, as we sat together at her kitchen table watching the spring rain drizzle down the window. A bolt of fear shot through me as I tried to imagine standing up in public and talking about Lois on some unknown day in the future after she died.

'I'm – I'm not sure I can handle that,' I stammered.

'Sure you can.' She grinned and went right on, as if the matter were settled. 'I want it to be a service of joy and victory. Here is a list of my favourite Bible readings and songs.'

She opened a red folder of papers. She talked some more about programmes and music and finally handed me the whole folder. 'I know you can do it,' she said, adding with the slightest wobble in her voice, 'I don't want Don to have to deal with these details. I'm counting on you.'

I nodded numbly. We hugged and I went home.

Later that afternoon I sat at my desk, staring at the folder. I can't do this, I told myself. But today at least I can write down a few notes about our conversations. I did that and stuffed the papers into the red folder. 'Lessons from Lois,' I wrote across the front.

As the weeks passed, Lois grew weaker. When she could no longer walk to the corner, I pushed her around the neighbourhood in a wheelchair that we christened Her Royal Carriage. When she needed to carry her canister of oxygen along, we dubbed it 0-2 like some friendly character out of a science fiction movie. She delighted in our wheelchair walks and so did I.

Though the vitality was being sucked from her body, her spiritual strength seemed to be growing every day. 'Sometimes I'm still afraid of dying,' she admitted, 'but I'm not afraid of death. I know where I'm going.' Always, I came home from these walks and added more notes to my Lessons from Lois folder.

Finally the day came when Lois was no longer able to get out of bed. She became a hospice patient and a kindly nurse visited regularly to adjust her medicine and keep her free from pain. Her parents came from California. Don began to take more time off work to be with her. We all took turns sitting by her bed. Sometimes I sang songs or read to her. She told me I wasn't a great singer but she liked me anyway.

My last visit to Lois came on a Friday afternoon. I didn't think she knew I was there, but I sat on her bed, my face close to hers, and softly recited some of her favourite verses. 'You have fought the good fight ... finished the race, kept the faith. Well done, good and faithful servant.'

I moistened her parched lips with a damp swab of cotton. Without opening her eyes, she reached up and gently touched my face. 'You've done well too,' she whispered. 'Thanks.'

Lois died just before dawn two days later on a Sunday morning.

'Her journey is over,' Don told me quietly on the phone. Even though I expected the news, I suddenly had a hard time connecting the word 'death' with Lois. The two didn't go together.

It wasn't until the next afternoon that I pulled out my Lessons from Lois folder and began to spread the small scraps of paper across my desk. As I did I saw a pattern: clear, tangible evidence of how God gave Lois the strength to meet her challenges. A strength which came not before, but when she got to them. She feared losing her hair, but when she got to that point she joked about all the dramatic looks she could create with her new wigs. She worried about growing weak and staying in bed, but when that time came she seemed thankful and content. And when she neared the end of her struggle she grew more and more peaceful about letting go of life here and looking forward to life in heaven. God transformed her fears into strength one step at a time, just as she had said He would.

As for me, I didn't have the same courage to face death as she did. But dying was not my challenge. Walking beside Lois and meeting her needs was, however, and God gave me the strength to meet these challenges – one step at a time. My challenge was to write her eulogy. I picked up a pencil and began.

4

WHEN TRUST OVERCOMES DOUBT

A prayer is a wish sent heavenwards.

Phillip Brooks

MAN WITHOUT A PAST

by Stan Peterson

I sank back on the bed, struggling to remember something, anything.

In a strange way I was in fact twenty-three years old when I was born. My first recollection was staring at a stark white ceiling, my body throbbing with pain. Two blurred figures looked down at me. Straining to focus, I saw it was actually only one person, a kind-faced woman who was stroking my forehead.

'Son,' her voice broke, 'we've waited so long for you to wake up.'

I didn't know her. Nor did I recognize the others who tiptoed to my bed. The woman said they were my brothers and sisters. Who were these people? Why couldn't I move? I stared at the woman, bewildered.

'You have been in a coma for a month, son,' she said. 'You're in the Mayo Clinic in Rochester. Do you remember what happened?' For some reason her words made no sense to me. I remembered nothing, not even who I was.

The woman later explained that I had been driving down a highway outside of Rochester near my home when a speeding truck struck my car head-on. I was given up for dead, but an ambulance rushed me to hospital, where doctors revived me. My jaw was fractured, my left leg shattered, and a traumatic head injury had left my right arm and leg paralysed. In addition to this, I had suffered a complete loss of memory.

'Several times the doctors gave up on you,' she said, taking my hand. 'They told us you were dying.'

Each time they told her that, she would call my brother Rick, a minister, and people would gather together and pray for me.

'God answered our prayers, son,' she added, squeezing my hand.

As weeks in the hospital passed, I came to recognize my mother, brothers and sisters. When I asked, in a slurring voice, about my father, Mother showed me a photo. I did not recognize the grey-haired man. 'Your father died nine years ago, when you were fourteen,' she explained.

I stared at her in despair, and then sank back on the bed, struggling to remember something, *anything*. There was only blankness. Would my memory return?

In the months that followed, the doctors sadly shook their heads. 'Not with the severity of the head injury,' they said. 'You have total retrograde amnesia. The return of any memory is doubtful.' But when the doctors said I would never talk clearly or walk again, I was determined to prove them wrong.

Rehabilitative exercises at the hospital found me dragging myself along parallel bars until my sweatsuit was drenched. In speech therapy I forced myself to enunciate until my jaw was numb. Finally, after two and a half months, I was wheeled home.

'Home' was a strange place, including the room Mother said was mine. The photos and school pennants on its wall meant nothing to me. Neither did the framed diploma stating Stan Peterson had earned a Bachelor of Science degree.

I tried to retrieve pieces of my childhood, but the homemade model aeroplanes and the rusty bike had belonged to someone else. I pored over the dog-eared family photo for hours. Mother pointed out faces: Aunt Helen, Uncle Harry ... but they were all strangers, even the wide-eyed boy staring out from the trailer. Mother said he was me, at the age of seven. I put the album aside, feeling like an alien transmuted into a stranger's body.

Some residual skills came naturally; I could drink from a coffee cup and brush my teeth with my left hand, but I could not remember the brother who Mother said took me fishing. From time to time someone would attempt to awaken a memory. 'Remember when you played in the football team, and when you got the basketball scholarship for college?' I'd try and try, then shake my head. Me, running? Just moving around the house in a walker took all the strength I had.

Even so, I knew that to become a fully functioning person I had to learn to read. To begin with, I had to relearn the alphabet. It seemed impossible to grasp. But a first-class teacher tutored me, and as I struggled with the letters, vague associations came to me. Eventually I could read simple sentences in a *Dick and Jane* school book. I held a ruler under each line so my wavering eye could follow the words. Often by the time I reached the end of a line, I couldn't remember the first part of it.

Mother saw my growing frustration and despondency. 'Son, why don't you ask God for help,' she suggested, describing how family prayer had pulled me through my crisis. By now I had come to recognize God as my Creator, a powerful spiritual being. But I could not conceive of Him as someone to whom I could talk. He was 'out there' somewhere.

And so I continued driving myself – reading and rereading, forcing information into the labyrinth of my mind. Sometimes the assimilation was more than I could bear. Once, eyes smarting and temples throbbing, I angrily threw the book down, hoisted myself on to the walker and clumped around the house in frustration.

As I struggled from room to room, I found myself stopping in front of a picture on Mother's bedroom wall. I had seen it before and it always intrigued me.

It was of a bearded man kneeling in agony beside a huge rock. Pain filled his face, and I felt a kinship with him. Yet he also seemed to have a peace and serenity for which I so longed. Somehow I felt I should know this person. Who was he? I asked Mother about it. She was quiet for a moment, removed it from the wall and sat down holding it in her lap.

'It's Jesus in the garden of Gethsemane, son,' she said softly, 'where he spent the night before his crucifixion, praying to his Father.'

Mother had told me of this picture before, but seeing this vivid portrayal helped me visualize Jesus as a real person. I looked at that picture often during my long months of recovery and developed a close relationship with him. He was someone I could talk to, pray to, seek help from. Through reading his words in the Bible, I found what I needed in order to live as a man without a past.

'Behold,' Jesus said, 'I make all things new.' I began to see some good things in my condition. The past had no claim on me. I had no worries, no regrets. I had a clean slate. *Life* was ahead! Each new day promised new adventure.

In my enthusiasm I found myself doing even more than I thought possible. Every day I went to the public library, where a kind woman, who took pains to understand my hesitant speech and frequently wrong words, suggested new books for me to read. The walk was good therapy, and I graduated from the walker to a cane. People would greet me as I limped by. I didn't know who they were, but I appreciated their encouragement.

Each new book read, each lesson learned and each person met, were steps up my staircase of recovery. Months passed as I laboured over multiplication tables and worked through elementary books, each achievement stimulating my growing comprehension. Gradually, with the help of tutors, I moved on to high school subjects.

Then the time came when I was able to review my old college texts. Mother told me that before the accident, I was on my way to earning a Ph.D. at university and that I had planned to become a psychologist. I became determined to fulfil that goal.

Two years after the accident, I was again standing on the steps of the university. I had memorized the names and faces of the faculty from my college yearbook, but the grounds and the buildings were brand new to me. For a moment I hesitated at the entrance. Would I really be able to continue my studies? I looked around. Behind me was nothing. Ahead was everything. I took a deep breath, turned and stepped into a new adventure.

Sadly, I was not yet ready for the demanding doctoral programme. In class my mind would sometimes go blank, and in asking questions I would find myself at a loss for words. I became frustrated and thought I was going to crack up.

Then I learned of a psychology master's degree programme just beginning at another university. I decided to pursue that goal instead. Eventually I earned credentials in school psychology and became a consultant school psychologist for public schools. Later, I became director of psychological services and special education for schools. Eventually, I had my own clinic, working with the neurologically handicapped, and those with language and learning deficits.

Not until I began intensive work with brain-injured patients and stroke victims did I fully realize how wonderfully blessed I had been through my accident. My patients and I had both suffered similar disabilities, such as lameness, speech and vision problems, and memory deficiencies. The difference was that they remembered their past and desperately yearned to retrieve it; I had no memory of a healthy, whole Stan Peterson. So I suffered no longing to be what I once was. I could only look ahead. This had been my spur to getting well, to making a new life.

I found myself particularly drawn to people whose recovery was blocked by grieving over what they had lost. I recognized this syndrome not only in the brain-injured and stroke patients, but also in practically everyone who had suffered some kind of loss: men and women who had lost spouses, executives whose jobs disappeared through mergers, people grieving over investments that had vanished in the stock market. They, too, had imprisoned themselves in the past, 'If only I had made Bill see a doctor ... if only I had read the handwriting on the wall ... if only I had studied the market better.'

I tell these people to forget the past and, instead of dwelling on how things were, to look at how things *are*. The most important part of them has not been lost or damaged: their God-given inner spirit remains intact. If they look forward to the possibilities of what *can* be, they can still achieve a full life. It may be a different kind of life, true, but by building on what they have they'll be amazed at how abundant that life can be. Just as I found, the life waiting ahead can be a wonderful adventure!

THE YELLOW KITE

by Beverly Newman

Michael was the one spark of life left for me.

I stood at the window and watched the neighbourhood children flying their kites on the hill behind our house. My four-year-old son Michael stood next to me with his face eagerly pressed against the glass. Looking up at me, with pleading eyes, he again asked if he could have a kite like the other children.

For days now, ever since he had first seen them congregate on the hill, Michael had been asking the same question, and had been given the same answer: 'Wait until you are a little older.'

It was easier not to go into a long explanation, but actually Michael was too young to fly a kite all by himself, and that meant that one of his parents would always have to go with him to help. Because of my health I simply didn't have the strength or energy, and my husband was usually at work. Once again, Michael hid his face in my skirt, something he always did when he was going to cry and didn't want me to see.

As I turned from the window, I felt like crying myself. I looked around the room; the furniture was shabby and worn, and the walls were badly in need of paint. You could see the light patches, the places where previous tenants had hung their pictures. Even though we had lived here for several months, I had not done very much to fix the place up. We had moved so many times, and each time it seemed like the neighbourhood was a little more run-down, the house a little older, and each one in need of repairs.

My husband Bill worked long, irregular hours at his job and earned a good salary. However, there was never enough money and we kept getting deeper in debt. I had lost three children through miscarriages, and the complications that followed caused me to have to make several emergency trips to the hospital and to be constantly under a doctor's care. Consequently, a tension had grown between us and we found we could no longer get along with one another.

It all looked so hopeless; even God seemed to have forgotten us. I prayed so often about our problems, asking God for help, but things only seemed to get worse. I found myself thinking, God doesn't care, and I guess I don't either.

I walked over to the mirror and studied my reflection. It was almost like looking at a stranger. I looked pale and worn, much older than my years. I no longer bothered to fix my face or to do anything with my hair. I stepped back and studied my whole image – the old dress that I had worn all week was wrinkled and torn at the pocket and there was a button missing at the neck.

As I stood there and stared at myself, a feeling of dread, almost of panic, came over me; it filled my whole body with fear. It was the realization that I was giving up on life. I had stopped caring about anything, I felt defeated. I could no longer rise above the depression that had taken hold of me.

In the last few months, my husband had grown rather quiet and we did not talk much. I was aware of his eyes studying me when he thought I was preoccupied with something. I used to be so particular about everything. Bill had not said a word about the change that had come over me, but his actions said a lot. He had made a special effort to get me interested in new things, but I did not respond. In fact, I did not respond to him in any way, and he did not know quite how to handle me any more.

Michael was the one spark of life left for me. He could make me smile, and when he hugged me, I would feel love. I clung to him much in the way one would cling to a life preserver. He needed me and I knew it – that kept me going. As I tucked him into bed that evening, Michael said, 'Mummy, may I pray to God to send me a yellow kite?' Fearing that I might repeat what I had said so many times before, he added, 'Maybe He doesn't think I'm too young.'

'Yes,' I said. 'We will leave it up to Him to decide about it once and for all.' I was tired of the whole thing and hoped that maybe this would make Michael stop talking about it.

Michael prayed his prayer and fell asleep with a smile on his face. As I stood there looking down at that beautiful child with the blond curls, so trusting in his faith that God would answer his little prayer, I found myself questioning God. Would He really answer such a small prayer when He had chosen not to hear any of my frantic pleas or send me any help to relieve my situation? 'Oh, God,' I prayed, 'please help me! Show me the way out of this dark place.'

The next morning as I raised the blind in the kitchen, I stared at the sight that met my eyes – a string hanging down in front of the window. Not quite able to believe the thoughts that were being put together in my mind, I found myself running out the back door and into the garden. There it was, a yellow kite, caught on the roof with its string hanging down.

'Oh, thank you, God, thank you!' I repeated, over and over again. I was thanking Him for the yellow kite, and I was thanking Him for the joy that was flooding into my soul. He had answered the prayer of a little boy, just a little prayer, but by answering that prayer, He had also answered my own prayer for help.

Suddenly I remembered Michael. I ran to his room, scooped him up in my arms and carried him into the garden. He was still half-asleep and didn't quite know what to make of this mother who was babbling about something on the roof and saying, 'Wait until you see!'

He clapped his hands and bounced up and down in my arms when he saw the kite. 'Mummy, Mummy, and it's even yellow!' he exclaimed. I smiled at him and added, 'It's a miracle, too.' He hugged me and said, 'I knew God would answer my prayer. I just knew He would.'

When Bill came home we took the kite to the beach and flew it. It went so high that it was almost out of sight for a while. Bill said he had never seen a kite fly as high. We asked all over the neighbourhood but we never found a trace of the kite's former owner.

We moved several times in the years that followed, and the yellow kite always went with us. My depression left me and as my health improved, so did my relationship with my husband.

At each new place I would hang the kite in some corner where I could see it as I went about my duties. It served as a reminder that no matter how bad things may seem, we must never lose sight of the fact that God cares, that He hears our prayers. No request is too big or too small to bring before Him.

THE SOLUTION

by Joe Barbera

Tom and Jerry help their creators find a way through.

Hanna and I had worked as cartoonists at MGM for twenty years when we were let go. We'd produced an Academy Award-winning series of shorts starring the cat-and-mouse duo, *Tom and Jerry.* We had a good reputation and secure positions, but by the 1950s the movie studios were facing tough competition from the television industry.

Animated shorts seemed too expensive to make. One day in 1957, Bill and I were out on the streets. What were we supposed to do? I loved my profession, working with my God-given gifts, and wasn't about to give up. Bill wasn't either, so we joined our last names together with a hyphen. I drew and he was the mechanical wizard, a perfect combination. We figured we'd produce cartoons for television. There was one minor problem. TV couldn't afford us either.

We were horrified when we saw our first budget. Our sole client couldn't pay more than a tenth of what we were used to spending. 'The solution is here somewhere,' I said to myself. But what was it?

I did the storyboards at home, and my twelve-year-old daughter Jayne coloured in the drawings. We worked night and day, making progress. Still, neither Bill nor I could guess how to create a five-minute cartoon that normally took about 28,000 drawings on a budget for only 5000. 'The solution is here,' I said to myself again. 'I just haven't seen it yet.'

Bill and I looked at the problem from every possible angle. Then we remembered 'pencil reels', sample preview reels we'd pioneered at MGM to show our bosses what we had in mind.

In a pencil reel we didn't sketch each millisecond of Tom and Jerry's motion. If Jerry was running, for instance, I'd do just two drawings for the pencil reel, one with the left foot in front, one with the feet reversed. Bill would expose the two on film so that the legs looked criss-crossed, like scissors, and this image gave the impression of running. Is this the solution? I wondered.

We tried it and, surprisingly enough, it looked great. Quick, explosive, with the kind of action we liked. Our characters moved in a realistic blur of 'limited animation', a concept that eventually revolutionized the industry, making a whole line-up of Saturday-morning entertainment for children affordable.

What did I learn from the experience? When hope is hard to find, when I'm stymied by a problem, I think: I trust that the solution is here; I just haven't seen it yet!

A FUTURE AND A HOPE

by Lloyd Ogilvie

A gratitude for life filled my mind as I progressed down a country road, through woods, over rock fences and across the wide sheep fields.

The summer of 1987 had begun in a most ordinary, if somewhat scholarly, manner. I had travelled to Scotland to do research on a book I planned to write. A book on the subject of hope. Little did I know that I was about to go through an ordeal that would change my life and radically transform my theoretical understanding of this word.

For several weeks in the library of New College at the University of Edinburgh, I pored over everything I could find on hope. Then I reflected long and hard on what the great thinkers of all time had said and written about hope.

Sadly, the word 'hope' was seldom defined, leaving me frustrated and unsatisfied. It was a bit like listening to cheer leaders at a football game. 'Hope, hope, hope!' But the quality of hope was no more real after the cheering died down.

Finally, I crammed my notes into a bulging briefcase and headed north to a favourite haunt of mine on the rugged northwestern coastline of Scotland to reflect on my thoughts.

I was staying at a guesthouse on the coast, and late one Saturday afternoon I felt in the mood to take a long walk. It was raining, as it had steadily been doing for days, but that was no problem. I enjoy hiking in the Highlands in the rain. So I set out towards the boulders of the rugged seashore.

As I walked with leisurely delight, I was actually 'singing in the rain'. Gratitude for life filled my mind as I progressed down a country road, through woods, across a shallow, rock-studded stream, over rock walls and across the wide sheep fields. From there, I picked my way down a treacherous stone path to the craggy shore.

It was six o'clock in the evening.

Sheets of cold rain driven by strong winds beat on my face with invigorating force. Storm clouds blended with the sombre drabness of the sea. Waves crashed relentlessly on majestic rock formations that nature had heaped up along the shore. On a previous visit, I had enjoyed climbing over them to a vantage point where I could sit alone in quiet meditation. Filled with anticipation, I headed for that spot now.

I took a running leap and began vaulting from boulder to boulder with abandonment. Perhaps a new pair of Wellington boots made me overconfident on the rocks, made slippery by eight days of continuous rain. However, as I reached the highest boulder, I remember thinking, Lloyd, be careful.

Then it happened. My right foot began to slip. Skidding and off-balance, I felt my left leg plunging down between two boulders into a crevice so narrow it acted like a vice. As I fell to the left, all 180 pounds of me was levered on the imprisoned leg. My head bashed against the rocks.

I don't know how long I lay there, but piercing, throbbing pain stabbed me awake. I realized that the upper part of my body was on one boulder, my right leg on another and my left leg was pinned between the two. Painfully, I inched up until I could sit. Then I began the excruciating process of pulling my left leg out of the rocky vice. I was alarmed: the pain was almost unbearable and my leg felt like a limp piece of spaghetti.

When I finally freed my leg, I sat shivering in shock. After a time, I tried to edge myself up even farther, but the leg collapsed beneath me. My mind raced in panic. Nausea made me retch. Cold rain continued to drench me. I shivered, partly from the damp cold and partly from the physical shock my body had sustained. Alternately I felt burning fever and cold sweat.

Grim possibilities paraded before my mind's eye: what a dangerous, desolate place this was! Foolishly, I hadn't told anyone where I was going. Probably I wouldn't even be missed until dinner. By the time they could put together a search party, it would be pitch dark, and my chances of being found before morning would be slim. I doubted I could survive the night. Even in August the nights along the northwestern Scottish coast are damp and bitterly cold. Then, even in the pain and haze of the moment, an ironic thought flooded my mind. There I was, ready to write a book on hope, but now I was badly hurt and in an apparently hopeless situation.

Hope? Yeah, Lloyd I said to myself, what about hope! Where's the hope you've been thinking and studying about these past weeks? The hope you've tried to tell others about all through the years?

As I sat shivering in pain, a desperate strategy for survival began to take shape in my mind. I knew I couldn't stand up, let alone walk but maybe I could drag myself along on my back until I reached the country road. I had to try!

Bolts of pain shot through my leg when I made my first move. My body ached from the battering sustained in the fall. But slowly I edged my way off the rocks.

As I rested from the painful ordeal, I had the haunting feeling the situation was hopeless. I cried out, 'Someone, please help me!' An inner voice responded firmly, 'We're going to make it!'

In my mind's eye I pictured the long way back up the steep hill, over the stone walls, across the sheep fields, through the stream, deep into the forest, and finally on to the main path. All you have to do, the inaudible voice said, is put your arms and hands behind you, flex up your uninjured right leg and push. Tuck your long fishing coat under your buttocks and slide. Don't think about the distance; just make twelve pushes and then rest. Push and slide, Lloyd, push and slide!

Following orders, I found that my heavily waxed coat did slide smoothly over the rain-soaked earth. At times as I made my way up the steep and slippery hill, I would slip back a foot for every two that I made. But I was making headway.

After each set of twelve pushes, I'd rest and pray and call out for help. When I reached the top of the hill, the worst was still ahead. Between the sheep field and me was a high stone wall. How would I ever make it over that? Don't give up, Lloyd; don't give up, the voice encouraged.

Bracing myself against the rocks of the wall and clawing tenaciously, rock above rock, I finally clutched the top of the wall. I pulled myself up until I could put weight on my undamaged right leg. Then I fell across the top of the wall and down the other side. Pain flashed through my entire body.

At the other side of the field was another wall. Same climb required. Deeper cuts in my hands. Another fall ... Fording the shallow stream on my back left my energies even more depleted. Any part of me that had not been drenched by the pouring rain was now soaked to the skin. My teeth rattled, as the cold seemed to penetrate every inch of my body. You can't stop now, Lloyd. Push and slide. Through the woods. The main path is just beyond!

By the time I made it through the woods to the path, I was drifting in and out of consciousness. In my lucid moments, I realized that my only possibility of being found would be by a passing walker.

After each twelve pushes and slides I would cry out, 'Help! I've broken my leg! Someone, please help me!' Silence. No reply. No help.

A question flashed through my mind: what if I didn't make it? I was not afraid of death, and I didn't make any death-road promises, but at the same time, I wondered, where is He now? Why doesn't He send someone to help? My mind drifted back over the past.

The faces of my family, friends and loved ones came into sharp focus. I sobbed with gratitude. Then all the plans for the future flashed across my mind ... Push, Lloyd, push!

My body screamed in protest; I couldn't move. My strength was depleted. Then a favourite verse of hope from the Bible raced across my mind. I had memorized it years before: 'For I know the thoughts that I think towards you, says the Lord, thoughts of peace and not of evil, to give you a future and a hope.'

As I lay there, I thought about that amazing assurance. Strangely, during that time of prayer, the rain stopped. About half an hour later, in the distance I saw three people leisurely walking along another path. My pulse beat faster as I called out to them with a raspy voice. They didn't hear me at first, and I tried desperately to shout louder. Finally they turned and walked in my direction. As they got closer, I could see that they were a middle-aged man and two teenagers, a boy and a girl.

'Please help me,' I pleaded. 'I've injured my leg.'

'Don't worry,' the man said, kneeling down beside me. 'I'm a doctor. Now let me look at that leg.'

With trained hands, he took hold of my injured left leg. I shrieked with pain. I told him what had happened. I added how thankful I was that he 'happened' to come along the path. 'You're an answer to prayer!' I said.

The doctor smiled warmly and said that he too sensed the propitious timing of his evening walk. Then he introduced himself and his children. He was a cardiologist from Edinburgh. He and his family were on holiday, staying in a nearby cottage. They had decided to take a walk that evening when the rain stopped.

'Good thing we found you,' he said, 'you're in extreme pain and shock. You would probably not have made it through the night.' Leaving me with his son, the doctor and his daughter ran off to fetch a farmer who had a Land Rover.

As I waited, I checked my watch; it was 8.45 p.m. I had been dragging myself for two hours and forty-five minutes. Why had God taken so long to send help? Even in the fog of my pain, somehow I knew the answer. It was when I gave up and surrendered the seemingly impossible circumstances to the Lord that I made one of the most crucial discoveries of my life. Authentic hope is born when we trust God completely. Hope is a Person. In those two hours, I had come to know Him more profoundly than ever before.

DEATH WAS MY BIGGEST FEAR

by Bob Morgan

I was hurled on to the track directly in the path of the speeding wheels.

To be a good stunt man you have to have three qualifications: good nerves, good physique, and a liking for your job. Of the three, good nerves are probably the most important, for every time you go to work you face danger. I have learned that a man's body can be broken in a few minutes, but in the past few months I have learned that a man's soul is a lot less fragile.

My career started a short time after I got out of the navy. Over the years, I have performed all sorts of hair-raising feats while carefully made up to look like one movie star or another – and I never got hurt. I never got hurt because I never took unnecessary chances and always kept myself in top physical condition. Like a boxer or a football player, I'd actually go into strict training three or four weeks before we started shooting a picture.

That's what I did before we went on location in Arizona with the cinerama epic, *How the West Was Won.* Everything went well until one sunny day in April when we were filming the train robbery scene.

The train was an old-fashioned, narrow-gauge affair consisting of an old-time big-funnelled locomotive, one or two passenger cars, several flatcars carrying enormous logs and a caboose. With my hair dyed blond, I was supposed to fill in for actor George Peppard in a risky scene where he clings to the big logs and dangles over the coupling between two of the flatcars.

The script called for the huge load of timber eventually to be spilled into a ravine, in a spectacular wreck. The chains that held the logs were designed to be released hydraulically at a given signal. The trouble was, and it was almost fatal trouble for me, that the signal was given too soon.

Having finished my scene, the cameras were still on me, and turning. I was between the flatcars, just over the coupling, when the logs were released. Fifteen thousand pounds of timber hit me in the back. I was hurled on to the track directly in the path of the speeding wheels. Two flatcars and the caboose went over my body.

I suppose people have fallen from moving trains, landed *between* the rails, and come out alive, but I was across the rails. I remember thinking, 'This is it. What a way to die.' One of the flatcars hit me so hard that it completely jumped the track.

When they picked me up I understand that I was more like a mangled rag doll than a human being. The right side of my face was torn away. My body was a twisted nightmare. Later, they took a piece of railing about a foot long out of my back. Nobody thought that I'd be alive when they got me to the nearest doctor at the local town.

I was, but just barely. My injuries were beyond the scope of a small-town hospital, so I was rushed by ambulance to the nearest major hospital, seventy miles away. Nine doctors struggled frantically to keep me alive, while dozens of pints of blood were pumped into me. Even so, the doctors later told me that my heart had stopped twice while they were working on me. Something they couldn't explain got it going again. I was also told that at that time a lot of people had been praying for me, and it made me wonder about the extraordinary and unexpected possibilities of prayer.

A SENSE OF HUMOUR

by Brenda Wilbee

When I opened the door to my bedroom, I laughed out loud.

Two years ago, I went to visit a friend, leaving my two teenagers home alone. Phillip was sixteen, Blake fourteen. Would they be all right? Would they get into an accident? What if something terrible happened at school? Would the house burn down? What if they trashed the house?

I returned home eight days later at three in the morning. The boys had left on a lamp, there was a welcome-home note on the counter, the house was in perfect order. When I opened the door to my bedroom, I laughed out loud.

There was a man in my bed! A pair of blue jeans had been carefully laid out, with dirty socks for feet. A T-shirt made up the chest. Rolled-up posters worked for arms, mittens served as hands, the head was a Bruce Willis book, propped against my pillow. A baseball cap topped everything off. And stacked on the T-shirt? A pile of presents.

Nothing untoward had happened. My boys had even missed me and gone out of their way to welcome me home.

ONCE IN A MILLION

by Frank Tripp

A judge without judgement.

Judge Fennell, one of the finest men I ever knew, was walking along the street one day near Central Station. His big, athletic hulk bumped into a man who was milling about among the horde of hurried subway moles en route to their respective homes.

The man, dazed by the impact, staggered backwards as if to fall. Tom, as everyone called the judge, caught him by the shoulders and held him up. The man was well dressed and sober but his eyes were wild and bloodshot. 'Let me go, I'm all right,' he said; but Tom saw that he wasn't, and held on to him.

Judge Fennell, tired from a long day on the bench, took the bewildered stranger into the nearby Commodore Hotel and induced him to stay for dinner. When the man talked, the judge learned that I knew him.

That very afternoon the same man had come to me in distraction. He was a well-known newspaper salesman who used to call on me. He had a good job then and earned good money. Everybody liked to have him around.

When he was about thirty-five he met a girl. She wasn't the right girl for him but he worshipped her. The home and family he wanted never came about. She was out too many nights with other men for that. He began to drink away his troubles, first now and then, but eventually too much. His work slipped. His friends avoided him, his contacts dwindled, and he lost his job.

When he came to me, he borrowed two dollars and wanted no more. The judge now found out why: the poor man only wanted to repay a loan he'd had from a friend. Then he was going to kill himself.

When Tom bumped into him, the salesman had just decided it should be the river, rather than the subway tracks he'd first selected. Tom Fennell, after verifying the story, went to work on him in earnest. Tom won. The man reclaimed his wrecked life.

Judge Fennell has since passed on, but I often think of him warmly and wonder how many of us, after bumping into a stranger as did Tom, would merely say, 'I'm sorry,' and go on.

And I wonder if it was just coincidence that in the great, heartless city of New York, this man who never had heard of Tom Fennell, happened to go straight from me into the arms of this grand fellow? Somehow I don't think it was just coincidence.

THE WOMAN FROM NOWHERE

by Laura Sowers

Somehow I felt I could trust this woman, even though she was a complete stranger.

My infant son Marc and I were shopping in a large department store. On our way down to the main floor, Marc hopped on the escalator. I followed. Suddenly Marc screamed. I'd never heard a sound like that before.

'Mum! My foot!'

Marc's right foot was wedged between the side of the moving step and the escalator's wall. His body was twisted towards me. He screamed again. The escalator continued downwards.

In the panic of the moment, the danger at the bottom of the escalator flashed before me, the thought of the foot being severed – 'Turn off the escalator!' I screamed.

'Somebody help! Oh, dear God, dear God, help us! Help us!'

Several people at the base of the escalator began a flurry of activity. The escalator stopped. Someone had pressed an emergency button at the bottom of the step.

Marc clutched my arm and cried while I struggled to get a better look at his foot. A chill raced up my spine when I saw the tiny space in which his foot was trapped. It looked no more than a quarter of an inch wide. All I could see of his foot was his heel. The rest had disappeared into the jaws of the machine.

'Someone call the fire brigade!' I shouted.

Marc looked up at me desperately. 'Mum,' he said, 'pray!'

I crouched next to him, holding him, and prayed. For a moment he quietened down. Soon, though, he began crying again. 'Daddy! Daddy!' he called out.

I shouted out our business phone number, hoping someone would call my husband.

The two of us sat waiting. Marc cried and I patted his head. As the minutes passed I could see dark images of crutches and wheelchairs. I had always taken for granted that our little son would grow up playing baseball and soccer, running on strong legs and sturdy feet. Now, nothing seemed certain.

Marc looked up at me and said, 'Mum, my bones feel broken and bleedy.'

I clutched his little blond head tighter to me, but now it was I who was feeling faint. I can't faint, Marc needs me. At that moment I felt warm soft arms enfolding me from behind and a woman's soothing voice calmed me down.

The woman had come down the escalator and sat on the step above me. She gently rocked me from side to side, surrounding my shaking body with a calm embrace. 'Tell your son his foot is all right,' she said in my ear. There was an assurance in her voice.

'Marc,' I said into his ear, 'your foot is all right.'

'Tell him you'll buy him a new pair of shoes – whatever kind he wants.'

'I'll buy you a new pair of shoes. Any kind you like.'

Marc's crying stopped. 'Cowboy boots? Like Daddy's?' We were talking about new shoes – new shoes for two healthy feet! For the first time since the ordeal began, I felt hope. Maybe, just maybe, his foot really would be all right.

'Tell him there are no broken bones,' she said.

Somehow I felt I could trust this woman, even though she was a complete stranger. So I reassured Marc too.

The firemen arrived. Two men with crowbars pried the step away from the escalator wall, at last freeing Marc's foot. His shoe was in tatters. It took all my courage to watch as the men pulled the shredded sock off Marc's foot, but when they did, they revealed a red, bruised, but whole foot.

I turned to share my joy with my wonderful friend, but all I saw was her leg as she turned the corner at the top of the escalator. I never even saw her face.

My husband, Craig, arrived just as the firemen were setting Marc down on the floor. He was still sobbing, but he could wiggle his toes. Later, X-rays confirmed what I already knew: no broken bones, only bruises and swelling.

To this day I do not know who the woman who helped me was. Many people have suggested that the woman was an angel. I can't be sure about that, but of this I am certain: she was heaven-sent.

TOUGH LOVE

by Gordon Dobson

'I won't go!' he howled ... 'You can't make me!'

We considered ourselves a normal, middle-class American family, a *good* family. My wife Michelle and I lived in a nice neighbourhood with our two sons, Gordon, fifteen, and Gavin, thirteen. The local schools the boys attended were excellent. We ate our meals together. We did things as a family.

That's why it was so hard for us to see what was happening to Gordon, even when the warning signs were plainly there. Psychologists call it denial. For a long time we denied that our son was using drugs, and his worsening behaviour was ripping apart our household.

It started with Gordon skipping classes. His grades plunged. We were called in for conferences at school. At home he grew uncommunicative, spending hours in his room, the door defiantly locked. He skipped meals.

When he did emerge he was often belligerent. He fought with Gavin, to whom he'd always been such a wonderful big brother. Yet it was as if Gordon was becoming a different person, someone we didn't know or even like. Still, we blindly refused to suspect drugs. Not our son, not our home.

Michelle and I are both dyslexic. Gordon too is afflicted with this frustrating learning disorder. We became convinced that dyslexia, along with the usual teenage upheavals, was the root of Gordon's trouble. It had to be that. So we decided to send him away to a special private school for dyslexic children. But Gordon was strangely infuriated by our plan. 'I won't go!' he howled ... 'You can't make me!' He stalked off to his room.

I felt bad forcing him to do something he didn't want to, but Michelle, and I, were determined to spare him what we went through as students. 'You're going,' I said angrily through the door and above the roaring music. 'And that's that.'

I practically had to carry Gordon bodily from the house when the time came. He cursed. He kicked out a window. He cried. Eventually we wore him down and convinced him he had to go. Once inside the car he abruptly quietened down and slept quite heavily the whole way there.

Gordon coped even more poorly at private school, despite faculty assurances that he was bright and capable of the work. He was suspended several times. Michelle and I were devastated. *What is going wrong?* I'd lie awake at night wondering. When Gordon visited home he'd hole up in his room, blasting music and burning incense, while we sat silently in the room below, burying ourselves in the newspaper, blocking out what was happening above our heads.

He rarely spoke a civil word to Gavin, who just couldn't understand what was happening to his brother. This was not the good son we'd raised and loved. Where had we gone wrong? Parents make mistakes, but what had we done to cause such alarming behaviour in our boy? The more we tried to help, the harder he pushed us away.

One night while I was on a business trip in Europe, I got a panicky call from Michelle. She was tremendously upset about the results of a medical Gordon had taken in order to attend a youth camp that coming summer. The examination had included a drug scan.

'He tested positive for marijuana,' she divulged tearfully. 'What are we going to do?'

I was stunned. Even though the fractured pieces of Gordon's puzzling behaviour began to tumble into place before I hung up the phone, I was nonplussed. How many times had we warned him against drugs? How many times had Gordon promised he'd never try them?

There was nothing to tell Michelle but to sit tight until I came home. The rest of that trip is a blur. When I got back I lost no time confronting my son. I was frantic to get this thing out in the open and to deal with it.

'You tested positive for marijuana in your physical, Gordon,' I said, my voice squeezing out the words. His eyes widened slightly, he'd been caught. Then he smiled. 'Okay, Dad.' He took a deep breath, 'I tried it once, and I suppose it was still in my system.'

Silence. I fumbled for what to say next. 'I'll never try it again,' he offered. Our eyes locked. Suddenly I knew he was lying. He knew I knew he was lying, but Gordon stuck to his guns. I could not believe that my own son was lying so effortlessly to my face about using marijuana.

Finally he just climbed the stairs to his room and closed the door. Michelle and I talked with our doctor, and then made the decision. We would have Gordon treated in a drug rehabilitation centre. We'd been blind for a long time; now we wanted to do everything to stop the problem before it got any worse.

But it was already too late. At the rehab Gordon admitted to taking not only marijuana but also uppers, downers, PCP, cocaine, LSD and a list of other substances we'd never even heard of. *Our son was a drug addict*. Suddenly so much made sense: the moodiness and hostility, the grades, the wild rage at going off to a new school away from his drug source, the occasional missing money we couldn't explain – all of it. It all made terrible, shocking sense.

A counsellor forced us to confront the grim statistical reality of our situation, a reality we could no longer deny: 'There are thirty-six kids in this unit,' she said carefully. 'In five years, twelve will be off drugs, twelve will still be using and twelve will be dead.' Later we sat in our parked car and cried.

'Please, God,' I prayed desperately, 'please don't let my child die.' Gordon would need six to eight weeks of intensive in-patient therapy, they said, at a cost of nearly £400 a day. Our private health insurance covered only thirty days. 'How will we ever manage?' I asked Michelle on the way home. She just stared out of the car window. Neither of us had an answer.

We consulted a banker friend from church about a second mortgage.

It proved unnecessary. Two days before our insurance ran dry Gordon was kicked out of rehab for fighting with the staff. Back home again he retreated to his room, isolating himself more than ever. The company and the hours he kept, worried us sick. We never knew what he was going to do next.

We read books and joined self-help groups. We prayed. We cried. We got angry. We prayed harder. But Gordon didn't change. There seemed to be nothing more we could do for him. We had read a lot about 'tough love', how we had to stop blaming ourselves for Gordon's problems. We had to think about Gavin and what Gordon was doing to his brother's home life. We had to stop letting Gordon's addiction wrench apart our whole family.

Finally Michelle and I had no choice but to go hard on him. We'd reached the end of our fraying rope. We'd tried everything. Looking Gordon straight in the eye, I said, 'In one month you'll be retested for drugs. If you flunk you'll have the option of going into treatment, or leaving home for good, or until you kick drugs.'

I paused, wondering if my words had hit their mark. Gordon glowered, speechless. 'From now on,' I continued, 'you'll be home by curfew or you'll sleep elsewhere. Same goes for meal times. This isn't a truck stop.'

'We love you,' added Michelle, 'but we don't like who you're turning into, and we won't tolerate it in our home.'

A month later, after he'd slept elsewhere many nights and missed many meals, Gordon retested positive. We stuck with the ultimatum. He packed an old knapsack and left, slamming the door. With all my might I resisted running after him.

The weeks that followed were painful for our family. Things fell apart. The demands of a new job put pressure on me at a time when I didn't think I could take any more. To combat the anxiety Michelle felt over Gordon's leaving, she took up aerobics, only to injure both ankles at class and end up on crutches. She became more depressed than ever. We had no idea where Gordon was, but we knew he was suffering.

Then, while riding his bike, Gavin had a dreadful accident. Michelle called me from the hospital; Gavin had been taken there in a coma. I rushed to his side, frantic. The doctors could promise nothing. The only thing to do was wait and see if he came out of it, wait and pray once more.

'Gordon should know about this,' I said to Michelle grimly. 'He may have turned his back on us, but he still has a brother.'

The next day we cruised the streets and found him hanging out with some druggie friends. He was reluctant to talk so I minced no words: 'Your brother's had a bad accident. He's in a coma. We don't know what'll happen.' I searched his eyes for a flicker of worry, but 'You all right, Mom?' was all he managed to mumble. Michelle nodded. Then he turned and left to be with his friends.

We drove home in silence.

Early one sunny morning, a few days later, we heard a faint knock at our door. It was Gordon, deathly thin, weak, bedraggled. His vacant, red-rimmed eyes met ours. 'I'm ready', he barely managed to whisper, 'to go where you want. Take me today.'

We put Gordon in a drug treatment programme where he got help in fighting his addiction one day at a time, and where we too learned how to recover as a family. We didn't expect miracles. The simple realities of addiction had taught us long ago to expect neither good nor bad, but to accept God's will in our lives. Miraculously Gavin pulled out of his coma with no permanent damage. We still don't know exactly what brought Gordon to our doorstep that bright morning not long after the accident, but we know that somehow a power greater than his addiction drew him home.

The four of us will never be quite the same again. Drug addiction unravels the home, not just the addict. But in a way I think that recovery has made us a closer family, a family forced to draw on love to keep us from coming apart.

5

DISCOVERING HEALING THROUGH SICKNESS

Anyone can hold the helm when
the sea is calm.

Publius Syrus

A DREADFUL DECISION

by Dr Kenneth Swan

'I think you ought to know that the other surgeons feel you should have let that fellow die last night.'

It's odd, but I hadn't thought about him in years: the soldier whose life I'd saved in Vietnam when my colleagues said he would have been better off dead. In spring of 1989 I was being interviewed by a writer from a medical news magazine for an article on trauma care. I'm a trauma surgeon, and I told the writer about my experiences in triage – the process of treating first the wounded most likely to survive. That's when I mentioned my decision to save the life of the horribly wounded soldier.

A month later, after the article appeared in print, the writer, Peter MacPherson, called me with questions readers had raised, such as: 'Whatever became of the soldier?' and 'Do you think you made the right decision, saving him?'

'I don't know,' was all I could reply.

The questions brought back the memory of that night in 1968 in vivid detail. Fresh out of surgical residency, I was stationed at the 71st Evacuation Hospital, near Pleiku. I was having supper in my cubicle when a white-faced young medic came barging in. 'Doc, come quick!' Funny, I hadn't heard the helicopters bringing in the wounded.

The soldier was lying on a stretcher. He was so young – maybe nineteen – and had blond hair; a handsome kid, but all torn up and covered with mud, sticks and blood. To my amazement he was conscious, moaning over and over, 'Oh, God, I hurt so bad!'

A door gunner, he'd been on a helicopter that had taken a direct hit from a rocket, and he had taken the brunt of the explosion. I looked at his legs, arms, and the head injuries and couldn't hold back my tears. If the triage area had been filled with wounded awaiting medical attention, he would have been one of those shunted aside as least likely to survive. He would never have made it, but now he was the only patient, and it was up to me.

'Start IVs!' I barked. 'Get X-rays. We'll take him to the OR!'

During seven hours of surgery our medical team managed to save his arms, but we had to amputate both lower limbs and one finger. The neurosurgeon removed a large metal fragment from his brain. The ophthalmologist worked on his eyes, but they were beyond saving.

The next morning in the triage area the chief of professional services put an arm around my shoulder. 'Captain,' the colonel said gravely, 'I think you ought to know, the other surgeons feel you should have let that fellow die last night.'

I stiffened. 'I was trained to care for the sick and wounded,' I replied. 'God will decide who lives or dies.' He stared at me for a long moment, and then walked off.

I went into intensive care. Ken – I learned we had the same first name, was sitting up, swathed in bandages. He seemed remarkably tolerant of his terrible injuries, almost euphoric; I put it down to the brain injury. I began to wonder if the other surgeons had been right.

'Everyone wants him to die,' I wrote to my wife, 'yet I know I'll try to keep him alive.'

Four days later Ken was evacuated to Japan. A month later I learned from the chaplain's assistant that Ken had made it back home. Instead of being happy, I was despondent. If Ken had died en route, I could have consoled myself that it was for the best and I had done everything I could. That would have ended it.

But Ken was alive. For months I tormented myself with all sorts of grim scenarios: Ken immured in the back ward of a veterans hospital somewhere – crippled, blind, forgotten, more a vegetable than a man. He had come from a poor farm family. Perhaps he was being tended by his widowed mother in a dingy room of a ramshackle farmhouse, trapped within the stump of a body, maybe driven mad by neglect, bedsores and loneliness, maybe wanting to die and not being able to.

Now, twenty-one years later, Peter MacPherson was again raising those old questions, including, 'Can you find out what happened to him? If you don't want to, I'll understand.'

'No, I'll certainly try,' I said.

We began the search for Ken, but with one big disadvantage: I could not remember his last name. MacPherson searched the National Archives. I tried to find the chaplain's assistant who had told me Ken had made it back to the States, but to no avail. After six months our search reached a dead end.

Eighteen months later, in the autumn of 1990, when MacPherson was working on another article, he was shown a computer file from the Casualty Care Research Center's Wound Data and Munitions Effectiveness Team (WDMET). He wondered whether Ken's case could be somewhere in that vast computer file? He called me.

The name rang a bell – the WDMET had been at the 71st Evacuation. They ran around snapping pictures of our patients for war-wound research. I called the Casualty Care Research Center. Sure enough, Ken was in their records. At last! 'Can you tell me his last name?'

'No; sorry. Confidential.' He suggested I submit a formal request, which would be forwarded to the Department of Veterans Affairs for processing. I wrote the letter. Then came the Persian Gulf war, and as an Army reservist I packed my bags – still not knowing Ken's whereabouts – and flew to the Middle East, where I tended the wounded in Kuwait and Iraq, and lectured on trauma care.

Shortly after I returned home in the summer of 1991, I finally got a call in response to my letter. Ken was indeed alive, the caller said, and living in the South. 'His last name is McGarity. He is married and has two children, and he plays the piano and trumpet, and he scuba dives.'

'You've got the wrong guy,' I said. 'This man is blind, he has no legs.'

'No, this is the right guy. We'll send you more information.'

On 25 September 1991 – nearly twenty-three years to the day after that fateful surgery – I flew down to Columbus, Georgia, accompanied by Peter MacPherson and a photographer. We were all pretty apprehensive. After our two-and-a-half-year search, this was the big moment. At the Columbus airport we rented a car and drove out to Ken's house, which was in a comfortable, suburban neighbourhood. It was a lovely autumn day. I rang the bell. A woman's voice said, 'Coming!'

Theresa McGarity opened the door.

All these years I had pictured Ken as a slim, handsome young guy with blond hair. The man in the wheel chair behind his wife was stocky and balding. He wheeled right up and in a strong voice said, 'Hi, Doc!' He extended his hand. I shook it. His grip, in spite of his missing finger, was strong. He was jocular, even cheerful.

Theresa brought coffee. We talked. That afternoon, I was amazed to discover that not only had Ken learned to play the piano by ear, but he had changed nappies, babysat his two daughters and fixed flat tyres (although he couldn't drive the family car). He had even climbed up to fix the roof.

'I've cut down trees and done carpentry work,' he told us. 'Why not? There's a way to do all those things.' Theresa had encouraged Ken to swim – even without legs his body was quite buoyant – and together they learned to scuba dive. As if all this weren't enough, Ken had also gone back to school and got his diploma, then he'd completed a year and a half of college. He enjoys history, particularly wars and military strategy.

What, we wondered, had motivated him to accomplish all this, given his terrible injuries. 'When I woke up,' he explained, 'I was on a surgical flight back to the States. It was 4 October, 1968, my twentieth birthday. I knew I was hurt – hurt bad. I was blind and had no legs. But I also thought of all the things in the world I wanted to experience, all the adventures I wanted to have, all the things I wanted to learn about. I thought, 'Hey, I can't give all that up just because of this! Then I would have no life at all. That would be crazy! I can still feel the wind blowing on my face, the sun warming my skin, the cold. I can hear sounds, voices, music ... '

Not everyone was as optimistic as he was. When he got to a VA hospital in Chicago, he overheard a psychiatrist say, 'Why did they let this kid live? What am I supposed to do with him?' Somehow those comments only made him determined to prove the doubters wrong.

Ken met Theresa at an annual picnic of citizens band radio enthusiasts. They had talked a few times on their CBs. Theresa was nineteen, from a churchgoing family and fresh out of high school. She wasn't bothered by Ken's disabilities. Her grandmother was blind, and one of her Sunday school friends had cerebral palsy and was in a wheelchair. She loved Ken's way of interjecting humour into any situation, even his own. Though blind, Ken insisted he could 'see' Theresa's heart – that she was innocent and honest, and from a loving family. They were married just four months after they met.

Theresa looked at me and said, 'I always wanted to meet the man who saved Kenneth's life – to thank him for these twenty wonderful years and for our two beautiful daughters. The decision you made that night – how long did it take, fifteen seconds? That one decision is responsible for my whole world – for the life of the man I intend to grow old with.'

So I hadn't made a mistake in saving Ken's life. What I said to my superior that morning after Ken's surgery was true: 'I was trained to care for the sick and wounded. God will decide who lives or dies.'

And Ken McGarity, patriot, hero, husband, father and friend, is living proof of that.

ANGELS AMONG US

by Susan Grezel

How could I have fallen asleep before making absolutely sure she was comfortable?

Our eight-year-old daughter Autumn hadn't slept well in days. She was suffering from a bad case of chicken pox, and her temperature had soared to 104. Her skin was covered with itchy red patches that she was trying her best not to scratch.

That night I went to her bedroom. 'Honey, I want you to sleep downstairs, so I can hear you if you need me,' I said. 'Daddy's got the couch all ready.'

In the living room I tucked her in, covering her with an Afghan blanket. I gently stroked Autumn's head. God, please comfort her tonight, I asked as I stifled a yawn.

Exhausted, I went straight to bed myself. As I slid between the cool, smooth sheets and rested my head on the pillow, I realized I had forgotten to put a top sheet over Autumn. The Afghan could aggravate her skin, I worried, half asleep. I should get up. With my toes I could feel the fresh, clean, folded sheet I had set out at the foot of my bed. I'll get up and cover her ...

My eyes opened with the sunrise the next morning. Autumn! How could I have fallen asleep before making absolutely sure she was comfortable? I rushed into the living room, feeling awful. Leaning over my still sleeping girl, I pressed my cheek to her forehead. Her fever had broken! As I pulled the Afghan away from her face, a piece of white sheet peeked out from underneath. Relieved, I went to make breakfast.

'I'm glad you covered Autumn with the sheet after I went to bed,' I told my husband when he came into the kitchen.

'I didn't,' he replied. 'I went to bed right after you. You were out like a light.'

'But Autumn couldn't have done it herself.'

Just then she dashed in, bright-eyed. 'Hi, sweetie,' I said. 'Did you sleep well?'

She nodded. 'At first I was uncomfortable, but then something funny happened.' Autumn looked at her father, then back at me. 'A white light filled one corner of the living room. I wanted to get up and touch it but I was too tired. Then my skin felt cool, not itchy, and I fell asleep!'

Autumn grabbed a piece of toast from the table. 'Do you think an angel came to tuck me in?'

THE HIGHEST GIFTS

by Charles Allen

I had to forget about useless if onlys, and had to learn to forgive myself for my foolish mistake.

At 11.43 p.m. on the night of 12 November 1982, my life seemed almost too perfect to be true. Aged thirty-two, I was a successful young lawyer married to Ayn, my childhood sweetheart. We had two enchanting little boys: Lee, six, and Matthew, almost four. We had just moved into a fine new home. I was full of energy and ambition. My confidence in myself was unbounded. All this I had at 11.43 that damp autumn night. At 11.44 I had nothing.

Ayn and I had had dinner with friends. On the way home we stopped for a nightcap. At our house the young man who babysat for us had parked his motorcycle outside. Feeling adventurous, I suggested that he give me a ride around the block. Somehow we failed to make a turn and ran into a ditch. I landed in such a way that my spinal cord was irreparably damaged; I could not move or speak or breathe.

When an ambulance took me to the hospital, Ayn was told that unless a tracheotomy was performed immediately I had only minutes to live. An opening was made and a tube inserted into my throat, but my diaphragm was paralysed. I could breathe only with a ventilator.

For six weeks I lay flat on my back, staring at the ceiling. I could move my head slightly, but nothing else. No hope of improvement was offered me. I thought my life was over; indeed I wished it could be.

Early in the New Year I was transferred to a special spinal unit. There I found skilled doctors and compassionate nurses, but the months that followed were a nightmare of fear and pain. I missed Ayn and our sons terribly. I could not speak. I had to have my lungs suctioned constantly, a painful and frightening procedure. I was tethered to the ventilator by a length of plastic tubing. It provided me with twelve breaths each minute, making a rhythmic clicking and whooshing noise. That sound was repeated more than 14,000 times each day, and I came to hate it. In the endless hours a host of futile regrets paraded through my mind. If only I hadn't been so foolish. If only, if only ...

Gradually, with infinite effort, I learned to sit up in a wheelchair, and the first attempts at rehabilitation began. The long-range objective was to teach me to live without the ventilator. It was hoped that by having an electronic pacemaker attached to the damaged nerves that controlled my diaphragm, and by learning to use certain neck and shoulder muscles, I might be able to breathe again.

My progress was agonizingly slow. I remember sitting in a circle with about forty other patients. Each was supposed to demonstrate the special skill he was learning. My assignment was to blow a soap bubble through one of those toy rings children use. But when the plastic circle was dipped into the liquid soap and held near my mouth, I could not exhale enough air to blow a bubble.

The first glimmer of light in the darkness came one night. Moisture from the ventilator tube had dripped on to the floor. When the night attendant, a tall black nurse, came towards me, her foot slipped in the puddle and she fell right into the bed with me. She was flustered, of course, and apologetic. But something about the encounter must have made an impression, because later she came back with a friend, an Oriental nurse. They began to tell me quietly that it was unlikely that I could find strength on my own to endure what I had to endure. They said that God would help me if I would accept Him. They were so sincere that at length I did indicate that I would accept Him, although I remember wondering if God would find a place in His heart for me. No bells rang, no lights flashed, nothing seemed to change, but I believe now that this weak and tentative decision opened a tiny door and let something through. That something was hope.

Near Easter it was decided that Ayn and the boys could come from Charleston and pay me a visit. I was both elated and terrified. How would the children react to the sight of their father, now a shrunken figure unable to move hand or foot? I knew that Ayn had been having a very hard time, enduring great uncertainty, having to act as both parents to our sons. When they came into the room where I sat, all of us – doctors, nurses, everyone – burst into tears.

The boys got over the shock of seeing me, but Ayn was at the end of her resources. She had an emotional breakdown. In a few days she seemed to recover, but this was the first indication that perhaps our marriage would not survive.

Science has been able to do wonderful things for disabled people. In my case, an electric wheelchair was designed capable of containing the ventilator. By blowing into a highly sensitive mouthpiece, I could move the chair and guide it. A hard puff would send me forward; a softer puff would turn the chair to the right. A strong sip would move me backwards, gentler sips turn me to the left.

By August it was thought I might be ready for a visit home, but my stay went badly. I was a burden to everyone and I knew it. Under the strain, Ayn became silent and withdrawn. If we had had the wisdom to commit our problems to God, our marriage might have survived, but we didn't, and eventually in 1985 I moved to a flat where my devoted attendants continued to take care of me. In 1986 Ayn and I were divorced.

In some ways these were the darkest days. My old law firm sent word they could no longer keep me on the payroll. I think I would have given in to despair had it not been for one man, Henry L. Scott. 'Renny', as we called him, was rector of the nearby St Philip's Episcopal Church. Every Wednesday afternoon for the next year and a half, Renny came to visit me, and his congregation offered prayers and financial help.

By now I was free of the hated respirator, but that was not the crucial thing. The crucial thing was that Renny, with his quiet spiritual strength, made me see that acceptance was the key to my problems, acceptance with faith in the goodness and mercy of God. I had to forget about useless if onlys. I had to learn to forgive myself for my foolish mistake. I had to grasp the shining truth that those of us confined to beds or wheelchairs or solitary rooms still possess gifts of the highest order. We can show love. We can display humour, courage, friendliness, and godliness, unencumbered by the demands placed on the able-bodied. Renny made me see that while I could not throw a baseball with my sons, I could be a better father to them in many ways because my old materialism and ambition could no longer come between us.

In the autumn of 1987 the suggestion was made that perhaps I could use my legal training and experience to function as a judge in our local traffic court. Many people had doubts, knowing that I would have to sit in my wheelchair, that documents would have to be held where I could read them, that participants might be taken aback by a judge who could move only his head and who had to guide his wheelchair by blowing or sipping on a mouthpiece, but the decision was made to give it a try.

I'll never forget that first day in traffic court. I was frightened and the courtroom was packed. There was no ramp up which I could guide my wheelchair to the judge's bench. There was no amplifier for my weak voice. Nervousness made me steer badly; when one wheel struck the door frame as I entered the court, there was a collective gasp of dismay from the onlookers. Somehow I prayed my way through and today, more than two years later, I have no difficulty in handling up to 150 cases in one session.

Another great expansion in my life took place when I decided to join a prison ministry known as Kairos, a Greek word interpreted as 'God's special time'. Together with dedicated people from our community, I visit the prisons in my van, with its hydraulic lift for my wheelchair.

I go as often as possible. I try to tell the prisoners that while I am confined to a wheelchair, and they are confined behind bars, it truly is possible to break through walls of loneliness or bitterness, and that a merciful God stands ready to help us do just that. It is a joyous and thrilling thing to see a spark of love begin to glow in the hearts of these men and women, many of whom consider themselves forgotten or discarded by their fellow human beings.

As for myself, I am busy, and I am happy. I hope I am helpful to those who come into contact with me. My boys visit me often. On

Saturdays we go to ball games or the movies or fishing. On Sundays we go to church together. One day, when Matthew was lying in bed, he looked up at me suddenly and said, 'Daddy, what's heaven like?'

I thought for a moment, and then said, 'Son, when I die, that wheelchair over there will be left standing wherever it is. I won't be in it. I'll be in heaven waiting for you and Lee, and we'll pass footballs and play basketball and play tag. When we get tired, we'll call a time-out. We'll hug one another and tell funny stories and laugh for ever. And the Lord will look at us, and he'll smile and say, "Those Aliens are the ball-playingest people I've ever seen!"'

Yes. I'm sure of it. That's the way it will be.

HEAVENLY TRUTHS

by Adam DePrince

Cubby is truly a funny child. He is just naturally that way.

In 1985 I was given the choice to allow another brother to enter my life. Cubby entered bringing trust, humour and love. Now, five years later, I am being given no choice about his leaving. Cubby has AIDS.

It was Christmas week when my parents were asked to consider the adoption of two preschoolers with haemophilia. As one administrator put it, 'You already have so many haemophiliacs, why not two more?'

My mum, my younger brother, Erik, and I had all been born with a rare bleeding disorder, the control of which required transfusions of a frozen, concentrated blood product. In 1980 we had adopted Mickey, a baby with a severe case of classic haemophilia. He required frequent infusions of a different blood product. Intravenous equipment and syringes were as common around our house as spoons and forks in any ordinary household. What difference would two more beds and a few more cases of clotting factor make?

To be fair to the entire family, my parents felt that we should all be in agreement about the adoptions. I had always enjoyed my role as a big brother. I looked forward to the arrival of our new family members, Cubby and Teddy. I have chosen to tell the story of Cubby, my youngest brother, whose real name is Charles.

Cubby is truly a funny child. He is just naturally that way. He is also naturally loving and trusting. It is my funny and poignant experiences with Cubby that I store away in my memory.

A couple of days after he was placed with us I asked four-year-old Cubby to get dressed so that he could help me shovel the snow off the driveway. Proud that a teenager had asked for his help, he scurried off to get changed.

He came downstairs dressed in a T-shirt and shorts, convinced that shorts were proper attire for the weather. He was bewildered when I explained that it was cold outside. He insisted that it was warm. I scooped him up in my arms and carried him to the front steps in order to end his confusion. It was plain to see by the astonished look on his face that Cubby had not experienced central heating in his early years.

The fact that Cubby was brown – actually very brown – and we were white was a positive issue in our family. We told him that he was as brown and handsome as a little bear cub. This pleased him immensely. It was this outlook that led to a hilarious misunderstanding during a camping trip when Cubby was five. While in the public bathroom at the campsite, he struck up a conversation with another camper. The elderly man asked Cubby if he liked sleeping on the ground. Somehow Cubby thought the man had asked, 'Do you like being brown?' 'Oh, yes,' Cubby replied, 'I like being brown.' Perplexed, the gentleman repeated his question. Cubby repeated his answer. I decided that these two were never going to close the communication gap and whisked Cubby out the door while he was cheerfully affirming his pleasure over his complexion.

The following summer, while on a backpacking trip Cubby was concerned about the fact that I had to carry so much more than he. Without warning he decided to help me carry my seventy-pound pack down a trail. I had stopped for a drink from my canteen when Cubby caught hold of the frame of my pack and proudly headed down the slope. The pack weighed thirty pounds more than Cubby, so it dragged him down the path and nearly over a cliff as I frantically chased after him.

Last autumn I went for a walk with Cubby and our dog, Stripe. Because of the incline of the hill near our home I had to help Cubby along by pushing his scooter from behind. As I was struggling with the scooter I began to feel bad that I had not noticed before that its wheels were very tight. Cubby wears a full leg brace due to the ravages of haemorrhages in his knee joint. I wondered how he was able to ride the scooter around. At the top of the long, exhausting hill Cubby turned to me and said, 'Adam, I was afraid that you might let the scooter roll backwards, so I held the brake all the way up to help you.'

Now that Cubby's condition is worsening, death is an issue he must confront. He knows that he has AIDS. To avoid the topic would be cruel. He has told me that he is glad that we told him the truth. Now he has time to plan what he wants to do with his very short life. He is also pleased that he can prepare to face death without being 'in a panic' on his deathbed.

Death is impossible to deal with if there is no God. Without God, death is not only terrifying for the person dying, but it also creates an unfillable void in the lives of those left behind. While I was on a walk with Cubby one day, he asked me questions about heaven. I was deeply touched that this nine-year-old would put so much trust in me.

As much as I preferred not to discuss death, I knew I could not let my brother down. I explained to him that life does not end with death. Passing on to heaven is another, and better, part of life. If we are not afraid of being born, then we should not be afraid of dying. I told Cubby that in heaven there is no suffering and that we live with God. Cubby was comforted to know that there is no haemophilia, crippled legs or AIDS in heaven. But he was still concerned about missing his family. I reminded him that if there was no suffering, then how could there be homesickness?

We decided that time must be different in heaven. It must pass more quickly than on earth. That would definitely explain the lack of homesickness, wouldn't it? Well, at eighteen I'm not much of a theologian or child psychiatrist, so I must admit that I agree with my brother that pizza and the Teenage Mutant Ninja Turtles would surely be found in heaven. I also promised him that his permanently straight leg would bend in heaven, thus enabling him to fulfil his dream of riding a bicycle.

Cubby was worried that there would be a wait to get into heaven; such as there is at Disney World. I assured him that for him there would never be a queue for heaven.

IT'S WHAT YOU HAVE THAT COUNTS

by Linda Williams

By the end of the week, it was only the catheters and feeding tubes that were keeping me alive.

It happened at the dentist's office two weeks before I was to be married. I had gone in to have a wisdom tooth pulled. 'You don't want a toothache on our honeymoon!' David had urged me.

'All done!' the dentist said, bringing the chair upright. 'All done,' he repeated when I didn't get up. I couldn't move. I was hurried to hospital, where doctors attributed the strange paralysis to the anaesthetic used by the dentist.

Very slowly, movement returned. I remained in the hospital for a month, but it was six months before I could return to nursing school. David still wanted to get married right away, but I insisted on waiting. What if it hadn't been the anaesthetic? How could I ask David to take on a sick wife?

We were young; I was twenty, he was twenty-three. We could afford to wait. I completed nurse's training and got a hospital job. The paralysis did not recur. I sometimes had other ailments and problems, which were unrelated. Or so I thought. There were days when my vision blurred. Sometimes at the end of my shift my left foot would start to drag. 'You're just working too hard,' David would say.

We were married three years after our original wedding date. The following year Jennifer was born; two years later, Trisha. Was the string of complications – dizziness, kidney infections, ulcers – pregnancy related, as the obstetrician assured me?

Wanting to raise our family in the country, we bought a second-hand mobile home on fifteen acres of land, and I worked the 3 to 11 shift at the local Hospital in Portland, thirty miles away, leaving for work when David got home from his job repairing welding equipment. When I made my rounds, I began to notice that my whole left side often lagged behind the right.

I started losing weight so rapidly that the hospital shifted me to part-time work and put me through a battery of tests without arriving at a diagnosis. By 1980 I was down from 130 to 75 pounds, and doctors insisted on putting me in hospital. Two days after being admitted I woke in the hospital room to discover I could not lift my head, legs, arms or hands. As in the dentist's chair ten years earlier there was no response.

By the end of the week, it was only the catheters and feeding tubes that were keeping me alive. Around me the room darkened. Finally I knew when it was daytime only by asking the nurse. Then, as the paralysis spread to my throat, I could not even do this. Eventually a specialist confirmed that I had multiple sclerosis.

As a nurse I was all too familiar with this disease that progressively destroys nerves. I was thirty years old, and I realized that I might be dying.

After two months in the hospital I was to be released to a nursing home. Blind, mute, paralysed, I would require total care. David held my unresponsive hand as the doctor named several institutions. 'Have a look at them, Mr Williams, and let me know.'

'I don't need to look at them.' I heard David say. 'Linda is coming home.' And over the doctor's protests, home I went. I was sure that at the ages of six and four, Jennifer and Trisha would be terrified by the forest of tubes, but I heard only excitement in their voices: 'Mummy's home!'

Mummy? What kind of mother could I be as I waited for death in that little mobile home? Attended by nurses the health insurance paid for, I lay week after week, unable to move or see or speak, wanting the end to come quickly. Worse than this, God, who had always been so close, now seemed a million miles away. I knew

God could heal because I had watched Him do so, for some of the patients I had prayed for. When I prayed about my own health, there was no answer.

You have health. Use it.

I had what? Where had such a ludicrous thought come from? Certainly not from me. I was sick. Helpless. Why, the only part of my body I could move at all was a single finger on my right hand!

Then move that finger.

There in the dark, I moved that one finger. A mere quiver, but I moved it. Next day, and the next, and the one after that, I took my mind off all I could not do and focused it on that responsive muscle. Physically it was a movement of centimetres, but in my understanding, a journey of light years. Instead of bombarding heaven for healing, I was to concentrate on the health I had.

Hearing, for example! I could hear the wind in the firs, the chatter of the girls as they dressed their dolls. Thought! I could reason. I could pray, thanking God for husband, for children, for Himself.

What could a single finger do? Gesture a greeting when I heard footsteps in the room!

One day as I 'waved' at David in this way, a second finger trembled into motion. A week later I coaxed a few croaking sounds from my throat. Soon afterwards I saw one blur of brown and another of yellow beside the bed. The darker blur was Jenny's brunette curls, the yellow one, Trisha's blonde head.

As my sight improved and more muscles responded in my right hand and arm, I discovered an amazing range of activity in just a few inches. Jenny and Trisha developed an uncanny ability to make sense of my garbled speech. With the girls translating, I communicated an idea to David. Would he wedge pillows behind me till I was sitting up? Would he put my sewing machine on the bed table? And now, would he tuck the foot treadle beneath my right arm?

So it was that the girls and I began making their spring wardrobes. They cut the fabric and guided it through the machine, but I was the one who used the little mobility I had to stop and start the needle.

Doctors cautioned that such temporary reversals were not unusual with MS. A patient could improve, but sooner or later the disease might reassert itself.

I had stopped focusing on the disease, however, and was enjoying each gift of health. Like the time when, strapped in a wheelchair, I was first wheeled out of the bedroom. Like teaching the girls to cook. (They pushed me into the kitchen, and together we baked bread, and made soups and pies.) David built a ramp beside the front steps so that I could be wheeled outside. When growing season came, he mounted a foam-rubber pad on a board with wheels, narrow enough to be pulled between the rows of beans and carrots. Lying face down I dug my fingers into the damp soil.

Use the health you have, God kept telling me, and how many uses there were for each regained ability! Much as I had improved, it was obvious that I couldn't go back to nursing in a wheelchair, but there were so man things I could do. Parenting, for example, teaching, encouraging, and loving. When we learned that our church supported an orphanage in Guatemala, we asked to be considered as an adoptive family, and in 1984, four-year-old Sarah became ours.

Caring for a small child used every ounce of the health I had. And the more health I used, the more seemed to come. As Sarah grew older, I enrolled in foster-care classes offered by the social agency, and proudly heard our home declared ideally suited for nurturing children.

But MS was advancing again. Breathing was often a struggle, even with oxygen. Time after time I was admitted to the hospital, pronounced terminal, but survived to return home once more. To use the health I had was hard, as the pain in my abdomen became constant. A post-surgical patient is given 10 milligrams of morphine; by 1990 I was receiving 400 milligrams a day. In August 1992, when even this was not enough, surgeons proposed severing my spinal cord. This would mean I'd never walk again, but of course I couldn't anyway. Another option was to partially remove my digestive tract. As it had been eleven years since I'd taken food by mouth this, too, would make no difference.

My reason for refusing both procedures must have seemed ridiculous: I was convinced that God was still saying, 'You have health. Use it.'

A few months after the surgeons' radical proposals, our first foster child was placed with us. With my mounting handicaps I would never have attempted it alone, but our three girls were so eager that we went ahead. Already a veteran of twelve foster homes by the age of three, Brandon was a silent child who never smiled. It was a joy to see him soon turning into a lively, laughing little boy who could never get enough hugs.

One day I was wheeling about the kitchen getting Brandon's lunch when I heard an unfamiliar sound: the growling of my own stomach. I stopped, peanut butter jar in hand. Was it time to attempt some food by mouth? That day I sipped a teaspoon of watermelon juice, the next day a swallow of carrot juice. Slowly, I progressed to solid food, revelling in the forgotten, sensation of taste. And strength began returning to my legs. One day David walked in from work to find me sitting on the couch. He looked from me to the empty wheelchair where he'd placed me that morning. 'How ... ? Who ...?'

Eating. Walking. Driving a car. Coming off morphine. There was one addition after another to my inventory of health. As my healing has progressed, more 'problem' children have been entrusted to us: autistic, retarded, deaf. The evaluations that accompany each child are accurate, but not important. Unique, lovable, brave – there is so much more to say about these children.

I have discovered, you see, that it's not what's wrong with us that counts, but what's right. That's what I told the neurologist recently when he showed me the results of my latest tests 'I don't understand it,' he said. 'I see nothing but health here.'

'I know,' I told him. 'I've seen nothing but health too, for a long, long time.'

A GIFT AT SPRINGTIME

by Beverly Ruth

Each year, I had chosen seeds like a woman buying precious jewels. My gardening was almost an act of worship.

This was my second Braille lesson. Because of a congenital eye defect, my retinas had deteriorated to the point that I was legally blind. I felt like a foreigner in an alien world. My fingers fumbled over the stiff paper with its jumble of raised dots. My teacher, Jean Haugland, patted my hand and encouraged, 'Relax, it will come to you.' Her chair scraped back and her voice came from behind me: 'Have you talked with your husband about the mobility classes? Discuss it with him, Bev. I'm sure he'd want you to go.'

'What's there to discuss?' I jerked around to her voice. 'Look, I really think I'm wasting your time. And I'm sick to death of everyone telling me how much I can do, how being blind isn't the handicap it appears to be.' I got to my feet, my purse spilling from my lap. 'I might as well be dead!' I spun around and collided with a second chair.

'Protect your face!' Jean called, as I bent to retrieve my purse and rub my bruised knee. One of her first warnings had been to protect my face whenever I leaned over to pick up a fallen object. I wanted to storm out, but I had to find my purse. I groped on the floor for it, and then stood up and headed in what I hoped was the direction of the door.

In the outer office my husband took my arm. 'How'd it go?' he asked.

'Fine,' I lied, nearly dragging him out in my anxiety to get to where I would be safe and unobserved.

At the house, I sat on our back porch steps and inhaled the good, green scent of spring. The world was bursting with new life, but where, I wondered, was my own renewal? I thought about the flowerbeds and the vegetable garden I'd planted beyond the lawn each spring. They must be leaf-covered and full of weeds now. In contrast to my indifferent husband, I had been an ardent gardener. Each year, I had chosen seeds like a woman buying precious jewels. My gardening was almost an act of worship.

'Mrs Ruth?' At the sound of the boy's voice I jerked upright. I knew better than to jump up any more; bruises had taught me that sudden movements belong exclusively to the sighted.

'Billy?'

'I just came over to see if you wanted me to dig over your garden.' Surely he'd heard about my problem. Everyone in the neighbourhood was probably talking about it and watching me. 'I don't think I'll put in a garden this year. I ... don't feel like it.'

'Oh. Well, Mum saved some of the seeds from that special squash you gave us last summer,' Billy said. 'In case you wanted to plant them this year.'

I wanted this intrusive fourteen-year-old to leave me alone and I almost sent him on his way. Then I remembered that his mother, who was widowed and raising four kids alone probably counted on the money Billy made each spring tilling our garden. 'I suppose you could dig it over anyway, Billy,' I said with a shrug. 'Even though I'm not putting in a garden, it'll keep the weeds down.'

So he did the job. I sat on the back porch and sniffed the richness of the earth as the tiller churned it up.

A few days later Billy was back. 'Here are those squash seeds, Mrs Ruth. I bet they'd grow if you just dumped them on top of the ground.'

The plastic bag of seeds lay on my kitchen counter for several days. Just to get them out of the way, I took them to the garden, planning to dump them on top of the ground, as Billy had said.

Once outside, I began picturing where I had planted the squash last year along the back of the garden against the fence. Picking my way to the left corner, I stooped and pushed five seeds into the ground. Taking four steps to the right, I planted five more seeds. I did this five times, and then retraced my steps, stretching to keep my right hand on the fence as a guide, to make a second row.

When I came back to the porch, a voice said, 'Hello, Mrs Ruth.'

I froze in my tracks. 'Billy!' I snapped. 'How long have you been here?' He'd probably been laughing at me fumbling around out there in the dirt.

'I just got here. Mum said that you might have a hard time picking out seeds this year so she got you a packet. She hopes they're the right ones. And ... I brought you this.'

Billy placed a plastic pot, flat in my hands.

'What ... ?' My fingers touched some slightly sticky leaves. I fingered the blooms. 'Petunias!'

'I got other kinds too,' Billy said.

'What are they?' My hand brushed another flower. It came away with a distinct odour. 'Marigolds!'

'Right.'

Suddenly we were playing a game. With a few hints, I rightly named pansies, primroses and lobelia. They were flowers Billy had grown familiar with from seeing them in my garden year after year.

'Do you want me to plant them?' he asked.

I didn't have the heart to tell him that he and his mother had wasted their money. 'Yes. Just the flowers, and I suppose you'd better do a little weeding as you go.'

I would pay him a generous amount for his work, enough to cover the price of both the flowers and the seeds. To my surprise, he returned after school the next day.

'Mrs Ruth, I got an idea. Okay if I check out the shed?'

'Sure.' What now?

I heard clanking and banging in the shed and then he was back. 'Listen, I found a ball of twine and that bundle of stakes Mr. Ruth cut for you a few years ago. What if I drive stakes into the ground and run twine to mark the rows, and you can plant those seeds?'

He was so enthusiastic, I couldn't say no. When he had the first row staked and marked with twine, he handed me a seed packet. 'What is it?' I asked.

'Guess.'

Opening one corner, I shook a few seeds into my hand. They were sharp-cornered little rounds. I rolled one between my thumb and index finger.

'Carrot!'

'Nope,' Billy said. 'Guess again. Here are the carrot seeds.' He pushed an open packet into my hand. I put my finger into it and encountered much tinier, harder seeds. I felt the first seeds again.

'Radish!'

'Right! Hey, you're good. I guess being blind ain't the most worst thing that could happen.'

That was his opinion – he could see. But that was the way we went, guessing and planting and driving stakes and running twine. When the last seed packet was crumpled in the pocket of my old gardening jacket and Billy had put the tools back in the shed and left, I went into the house. After scrubbing my hands, I took out my Braille lesson.

Billy's 'Hey, you're good' still rang in my ears. What would he think if I read to him with my fingers?

An hour later I dialled Jean Haugland's office. That in itself was a feat I had not accomplished before. My hands were clammy as I waited, an apology ready on my lips. When Jean said hello, I felt like whooping for joy. 'Jean, this is Bev.'

'Bev! How are you?'

'Fine. When is that next mobility class?'

There was a pause. 'In two weeks. Are you coming?'

'Yes.'

'Wonderful. Did hubby finally convince you?'

'No. Well, sort of, I guess.' Explaining the timely arrival of Billy with his seeds and his persistence was too complicated, and besides, given half a chance, hubby would have talked himself blue trying to convince me to join the class.

'Jean ... I planted my garden today, and I just dialled your number without any help. I guess being blind ain't the worst thing that could happen to me.'

Jean laughed. 'It sure ain't.'

After we said goodbye and hung up, I went out and sat on the back porch steps. A light breeze brought me the fresh scent of tilled earth and new growth.

THE WOMAN WHO COULDN'T CRY

by Susan Holliday

They told me that I would never speak again.

By the time I turned twenty-two, I was pretty much a snob. I was mainly interested in good times. Appearances meant a great deal to me. In evaluating possible dates, I can remember confiding to my friends, 'He's not tall enough,' or, 'I don't like the colour of his hair, blonds are more my type.' My boyfriends also had to be athletic because I was crazy about sports. A new bowling ball was helping me edge up towards a 200 game. In high school I played on a girls football team.

The pace of my life accelerated after I finished school. Knowing I'd get bored sitting behind a desk in an office, I took a job in an aircraft factory. I was on my feet all day helping the mechanics, and I loved it. My spare time was devoted to whirling around dance floors, watching ball games played by my company teams on weekends and on vacation.

I went to church, too, but that was mostly because I had got into the habit and liked to be around the other young people who also attended. One Sunday morning in June 1969, I walked out of my apartment, climbed into my car, buckled my seat belt and headed for church.

I really don't remember getting into the car, I don't even remember going to bed the night before. My knowledge of the events of that day comes from my family and the newspaper accounts I read later. I was driving towards the church, a half-mile away from my flat. As I went through an intersection, a car driven by another young woman sped towards me. I had the right of way, but that was little consolation for what happened next. The other driver slammed into me broadside on the passenger's side. I was wrenched from under the seat belt and thrown free of the car into a rocky wall on the side of the road.

For the next three and a half months I was in a coma. Suffering from multiple fractures and internal bleeding, I needed electric shocks to keep my heart beating, and in one day I received a transfusion of eleven pints of blood.

'If Susan lives,' the doctors told my parents, 'you should be prepared to see considerable brain damage.' At best, they suggested, I was likely be a physical cripple and a mental vegetable.

I guess God had other ideas. For some medically unexplained reason, I pulled out of the coma mentally alert. Even though my mental powers were intact, my body had undergone a radical change. I had lost about forty pounds, I couldn't speak and I was unable to stop my legs from involuntarily thrashing against the hospital bed bars. For several days I kept thinking that I must be having a long nightmare, that I'd soon wake up and find I was the same old Susan Holliday. Then I'd blink and blink again, but the white hospital room would still be there.

Screams of frustration welled up inside me. I've got to say something or even moan or grunt! I'd think as I strained my throat and moved my lips. But no sound came out.

After a month of desperately attempting to mutter just one syllable, the maddening silence still held me. The doctors were pessimistic; they told me that because of damage to my vocal cords, it was unlikely that I would ever speak again.

Emotionally and physically drained, I finally decided to try prayer. Then I discovered that I didn't know how to talk to God. I fell back on an example I repeated in my mind, the first two words of Psalm 12: 'Help, Lord ... Help, Lord. Help, Lord.' Dozens, hundreds of times that day I turned those words over in my thoughts. Finally, that very evening, God responded. As I sat outside my room in my wheelchair,

I saw my doctor at the nearby nurses' desk and I somehow softly rasped my first words in over four months.

'Hello, Doctor Nelson.'

From that wonderful moment on, the incredible power of simple prayer became an everyday reality to me. Hardly an hour went by when I didn't talk to God about something. As I slowly learned to speak again, I found my vocal cords wouldn't always work. The words were there in my head, but by the time they had passed through my throat to my lips, the sound was often an unintelligible, slurred croak or grunt. And because I could only manage one, monotone syllable for each breath, it was hard to find anyone with enough patience and imagination to sit around and absorb what I was trying to say.

Friends from my church and members of my family did their best to communicate with me. But of them all, John Beaudry, a young man I'd known slightly from my high school days, became my most concerned and understanding companion. He surprised everyone by continuing to visit me almost every day. He'd come into the room and, like a big friendly bear, plant a brotherly kiss on my forehead. Then he'd say quietly, 'How're you feeling?'

Although I usually had to repeat each sentence several times to others, John seemed to comprehend everything immediately. We talked about trivial things, I can't even remember most of the conversations, but I can recall clearly how those tender, brown eyes of his would search my face.

In a way he seemed almost unaware of the seriousness of my injuries; he made it clear he regarded them as temporary problems. It was always, 'When you go back to work ...' or, 'After you get back on your feet again ...' His confidence in my recovery was infectious, and I began to find myself thinking the same way.

For some reason I couldn't explain at the time, I began to look forward to our comfortable visits more eagerly than any party or athletic event I had known before my accident. Still, I wasn't prepared for his words one afternoon soon after my late November discharge from the hospital. He came into my room at home and, looking very serious, said, 'I love you, Susan, and I want to marry you.'

My ears started ringing, and I caught my breath and shut my eyes. He had never hinted at romance. Except for those little pecks on the forehead, he'd never even kissed me. For a few moments I was silent as conflicting thoughts rushed in and out of my mind. More than anything else, I had always wanted to get married; but since the accident a gnawing feeling had made me doubt whether any suitable young man would ever want to take responsibility for someone with injuries and disabilities like mine.

Confused and upset, I responded lamely, 'I can't be sure right now, John. Give me some time to think.'

Thinking and praying became my primary occupation during the next two weeks. The accident may have changed me on the outside, but God was changing me even more radically on the inside. Even if I had wanted to, I knew I could no longer judge a person by his face or hair colour. John's loving nature obviously made him someone special.

Finally I said yes. Then things began to happen so fast that I could hardly keep pace with them. Strength slowly returned to my weakened arms and back as physical therapy taught me to roll over, sit up and crawl. And as summer approached, all my attention turned to preparations for the wedding.

Our church was packed that July day in 1970 when my dad rolled me down the aisle in my wheelchair. It was a beautiful wedding, and a lot of eyes were wet, but not mine. You see, another side effect of my accident was that something had gone wrong with my tear ducts. I couldn't cry.

As I embarked on my challenging, but frequently frustrating, new career as a handicapped housewife, I often wished I could fall back on the emotional release that tears can provide.

One day not long after we were married, I was sitting by the stove watching some meat simmer when I suddenly realized I had forgotten to add a sauce. I unlocked the brakes on my wheelchair, tediously wheeled myself to a cupboard, locked the brakes again and then, shakily, stood to get the sauce.

Then I slowly reversed the procedure to get back to the stove, hoping all the time that the meat hadn't burned. At the same time a pot of water started boiling over and yet I could only watch it helplessly as I struggled, with rising despair, to position my wheelchair in front of the stove again.

Peeling a potato sometimes took five minutes or more – peel, pause, peel, pause and pick up the dropped potato. Cleaning our house was an even more humbling experience. I would slide to the floor from my wheelchair and crawl as well as I could, dragging the vacuum cleaner behind me.

Making the bed was another major project. Sometimes I'd collapse into a heap on the floor, overwhelmed with my physical handicaps. Unable to cry, I could feel the emotion boiling up inside until I thought I was about ready to explode.

But God was always there, and He supported me and relieved my anxieties when I prayed, 'Lord, I'm so frustrated! Please help me. Give me a sense of peace, a confidence that your will is being done in my life.'

John's faith helped me too. As he watched me try to bring a bowl of salad to the table one evening in my wheelchair, I could see he was quietly confident that I was eventually going to make it. I had dropped the bowl before, and he knew I might drop it again. But he didn't pity me. He had the wisdom to be just firm enough to make me try to do things on my own instead of trying to do everything for me.

After I had placed the bowl carefully on the table, he said, 'I knew you could do it.' The affectionate look in those brown eyes – the eyes I had once thought would have to be blue – helped me understand how deeply he loved me despite my physical limitations. It gave me the incentive to try to clear the next obstacle, and the next, and the next.

Gradually strength and flexibility returned to my legs and arms. I found that I could hobble along haltingly behind a walker, and then walk by leaning against a wall for support. Before long, I was able to carry large bowls with both my hands.

But most wondrous of all, despite the predictions of medical experts that I could never become pregnant, I did. Our daughter Janine was born a year and a half after our marriage, and not even the painful pregnancy I endured could cast a shadow over the joy I felt when I looked into her sparkling blue eyes and fondled her soft hair. As I was recuperating from the delivery, John gave me a little book called *How Much I Love My Wife.* The sense of my blessings overwhelmed me as I sat there holding that volume. And suddenly, for the first time in more than two years, I cried – not tears of frustration, but tears of total joy.

I know now that the car accident I thought had ended my life was the best thing that has ever happened to me. I'm a different person – and all the changes have been for the better. Whenever I start to get blue, I think about the miracles God has performed in my life. I'm alive, I'm speaking much better and I'm very much in love with the father of our own beautiful daughter. I seldom need a wheelchair or any other support to walk, and I see marked improvements in my condition almost every day.

All of that has been the result of trusting prayer, and I truly have cause to shout.

THE UNSEEN VISITOR

by Lori White

The doctors could not encourage his parents to be hopeful, not after such a terrible injury.

'Be careful!' I called over my shoulder from the bedroom as my two sons, Jordan, five, and Hunter, three, made a beeline outside to play in the garden.

It was Friday afternoon and that weekend we were moving down the road into a larger house. My husband Chan had just pulled in to the driveway towing a rugged metal trailer that he had brought home from our family car dealership to haul some boxes and small pieces of furniture.

The house and garden were in complete disarray and the boys were having a blast poking around. But just as my friend Joyce and I started cleaning out the wardrobes, a sickening thud reverberated through the house.

'What in the world—' I started to say to Joyce. An instant later I heard Chan shout in a voice pinched with panic, 'Lori! Lori, come quick!'

I ran downstairs to the front hall. There I saw Chan, ashen-faced, holding a limp, unrecognizable figure of a little boy covered in blood. Blood streamed from his mouth, his ears, and from a terrible gash in his head.

'The – the trailer ramp,' Chan stammered. 'It slammed down on him when I wasn't looking ...'

'Dear God ... ' The boy wore green tennis shoes. It was Jordan.

'Lori, we've got to get him to a doctor.'

I snatched a blanket off the sofa and we wrapped it around the unconscious form. Joyce stayed behind to watch Hunter as Chan and I leapt into our car, I started the engine and the car roared out of the driveway. Chan grabbed the cellular phone and called 999 to have them alert our local hospital that we were coming. As we sped down the road we exchanged frantic glances and tried to soothe Jordan. Chan told him over and over again how much we loved him.

At the emergency room attendants scooped Jordan from Chan's arms. We watched helplessly while medical personnel worked over our boy. Just minutes before, he had been an exuberant child. Chan wrapped his arms around me and I buried my face in his shoulder. A doctor glanced over at us. 'We need to transfer him,' he snapped. 'To somewhere better equipped.' Equipped for what? I wondered, my whole being churning with fear.

Chan and I waited in the treatment room with Jordan and a nurse for the ambulance to take us to another hospital across town. As Chan signed some documents, I stood over Jordan and told him that no matter what happened, his daddy and I loved him and that we were praying.

Suddenly Jordan moved. At first I thought it was my imagination but Chan and the nurse saw it too. Then, slowly, almost eerily, Jordan rose up to nearly a sitting position, as if someone were gently supporting him with an arm behind his back. His soot-black lashes fluttered open and in a weak but clear voice he said, 'He's taking care of me.'

His eyes closed peacefully and he sank back down, motionless once again. The nurse looked at us in bewildered disbelief.

Chan half stood up, and a cry caught in my throat. We had taken our boys to church and taught them to pray, but usually they said their prayers at the table and at bedtime. Here was Jordan reaching out in a moment of terrible, desperate need. I too would have to reach out. Just then the curtains swept back and Jordan, Chan and I were rushed to a waiting ambulance.

The evening dissolved in a blur. As we arrived at the other hospital, Jordan was wheeled straight in for a CAT scan of his brain.

Chan's parents, Steve and Jane White were at our side, as were mine, Keith and Paula Turner. Other family and friends had got word and come. A minister, Rev. John Misenheimer, and people from the local church gathered in the emergency room. We were surrounded by people who loved us and prayed with us. Yet Chan and I didn't know whether our little boy would live.

Finally, the neurosurgeon, Dr Gregory Rosenfeld, spoke to us. X-rays revealed that the heavy trailer gate, had fractured Jordan's skull crushing fragments of bone into the area of the brain that governs speech, hearing and memory. 'There is no telling the extent of the damage', Dr Rosenfeld explained, 'until we go in and take a look.' It was only fair to warn us, he said, that the injury was very serious. As Jordan was sped into surgery I broke down and sobbed.

The people who had gathered prayed that the surgeon's skilled hands would be blessed and guided. The love of our friends and family flowed through Chan and me and an incredible, almost spontaneous feeling of peace and acceptance overpowered our fears. Six hours later Dr Rosenfeld emerged and, pulling down his surgical mask, motioned us down the hall to a room, and opened the door. 'Come and say hello to Jordan.'

Chan and I moved to Jordan's bedside. He was pale and his head was swathed in a turban of bandages. I reached out to him. Oh, Jordan. It was then I heard the sweetest sound of my life: a tiny burp erupted from my son, followed by a whispered, 'Excuse me.'

Not only could Jordan speak, but he still had his manners! By the time they sent him up to the Neuro Intensive Care Unit, he was asking the nurse for a toothbrush. 'The doctors don't know what to think about this boy,' she said. Still, we were warned that Jordan could take a turn for the worse at any time, and that seizures were a serious possibility with such an invasive head trauma.

Most worrisome, though, was the fear that his brain might develop an infection. Ahead of Jordan lay a series of intravenous antibiotic treatments to fight this potentially fatal complication. We were cautioned that the sessions would be painful for Jordan.

I stayed at Jordan's side all night but could not sleep. Once, near morning, Jordan moaned with nausea and everyone came rushing. I held him and he said, 'Mummy, pray with me.' Over those next few days, any time he was frightened or suffering, he said, 'Mummy, Daddy, come pray with me.' That was the beginning of a spiritual journey, with Jordan as my guide. The stronger his faith was, the stronger mine became.

Eventually Jordan was moved from the ICU to the paediatric wing, where the staff were eager to finally meet this 'miracle boy'. Shortly after his arrival a new therapist pulled me aside. 'Mrs White,' the young woman said, 'we need to plan your son's treatment. There's a lot of work to be done.' Confused, I said, 'I don't understand.' She checked her chart. 'Isn't your boy the one with the depressed skull fracture?'

'Yes, but he just got up and walked to the bathroom. He's been talking non-stop all day and he's building a house with his Lego.'

'That's incredible,' the therapist replied and went to see for herself.

The technician who had done Jordan's initial CAT scan also stopped by. 'I felt so sorry for you that night,' she told Chan and me. 'I never thought you'd get your boy back this well or this quickly. I wasn't sure you'd get him back at all. I've never seen anything like it.'

In fact, the only thing keeping Jordan in the hospital was the intravenous antibiotic treatments – a harrowing twice-daily ordeal that took thirty minutes for the burning, powerful medicine to be completely transfused into Jordan's body. Every time Jordan wailed out in pain he begged, 'Pray for me, Mummy. Pray.' And I would, as hard as I knew how. Poor Chan. After a while he couldn't stand to be in the room.

The ordeal exhausted me too. One night before the next treatment, while Jordan was sleeping, I felt as if I couldn't possibly endure another minute. Yet I knew he was counting on me. Kneeling by Jordan's bed I buried my face in his blanket.

The door opened quietly behind me as I got up and lay down on the bed beside Jordan; I wrapped my arms around him. When the nurse shifted his arm to put the needle in, he started to move. I patted him and whispered, 'It's okay, Mummy's here, and Mummy's praying.' He closed his eyes again.

Nurses stood by ready to help when the burning and crying started. The room was still and dark and hushed. Drip by drip the medicine entered Jordan's vein. Ten minutes. Twenty. Thirty minutes passed and it was over. Not once did my little boy stir.

The doctors were able to release Jordan after only ten days in the hospital. There was no sign of infection, and we brought him home to complete his recovery. He is continuing to heal, with only some loss of hearing in his right ear.

For a time Jordan didn't remember anything about the accident, but then one day while he was playing with a toy truck he suddenly said, 'Mummy, I pulled the pin out. That's what made the trailer ramp fall on me.'

I stopped what I was doing. 'It really hurt,' he went on, 'but then Jesus came.'

I tried to sound calm. 'What did Jesus look like, honey?'

'He was just ... all white. Then Daddy came and lifted the ramp off my head.'

The gate had weighed nearly three hundred pounds and Chan had said many times that he was amazed he had been able to raise it so easily.

'Jesus came to see me, when we got to the hospital, too,' Jordan continued. His delicate features were set in an expression of deep, unperturbed seriousness. A feeling tingled up my back. 'He lifted me up and hugged me and said, "Jordan, you're going to be okay now."'

My mind flew back, to that moment in the treatment room waiting for the ambulance to Frye when Jordan mysteriously rose up in bed, as if cradled by an unseen visitor, and spoke. Had he really seen someone at that instant, someone only a hurt little child could see?

I knelt and wrapped my arms around Jordan, and as I did I could sense another set of arms enfolding us both, arms that are always close when we are in need.

6

ON CONQUERING THE HURDLES

By perseverance the snail reached the Ark.

Charles Spurgeon

OUT OF THE SHADOWS

by Ellen Lawrence

The room filled with swollen blue monsters circling the cot, many monsters, but each wore the same face.

I did not want to attend the annual family gathering at hunting season, but none of my usual excuses were working with Ken, my husband of five months. I tried explaining my aversion to hunting: I couldn't bear the shooting of what I called Bambies. When that didn't persuade him, I complained that I was just too busy with work. Finally I pulled out all the stops and said, 'I consider hunting an ancient chauvinistic ritual and I don't want to participate.' I did feel that way, but that wasn't the whole story. I couldn't tolerate even the thought of telling anyone why I really didn't want to go.

Each year around 15 November my family – aunts, uncles, cousins and siblings – gather under one roof up north near the town where I grew up. The location changes from year to year, this year it was to be held at my mother's home. I had not attended in more than twenty years; that's how long the secret had kept me away.

But Ken was determined to go. It would help him get to know my family better, he said. Snow was falling when we arrived. My brothers hugged me and asked a dozen questions, which I answered distractedly as I frantically looked around the family room for the uncle I feared might be there. He had not arrived.

Relaxing around a blazing fireplace, the men told funny, exaggerated stories about white-tailed deer that got away. The women planned meals, played board games and laughed about 'the savage hunters'. Everyone had a favourite memory of past hunting seasons – everyone except me. At one point my eldest brother asked me, 'Do you remember the year Dad wanted to take you hunting?'

Our father had been dead several years. For a moment that scene came back to me. I was thirteen and loved it when my father took me along – anywhere. I remember his scratchy kisses and the sound of his laughter. His offer to take me along was a rite of passage. I was growing up.

By that age I couldn't stand the thought of being with the men during hunting season. As much as I wanted to be with my father, opening day sent shivers up my back. Now, as my sister, five brothers and half a dozen other relatives recalled past hunting seasons, I stared at the driveway waiting for my uncle to arrive. Once again my secret was robbing me. I couldn't enjoy the time with my family.

Finally someone said the uncle wouldn't be joining us this year; his vision was just too bad. Yet even without his presence, the memories were too strong. I excused myself and went to bed early. As I lay there in the dark, my eyes stubbornly open, I listened to every voice, every new arrival.

Next morning, in the pre-dawn dimness of opening day, I watched Ken pull on his bright orange coat and straighten his hat. As he leaned down to kiss me before leaving, he said, 'Is something wrong? You tossed and turned all night.'

Looking past him at the wall, I said, 'I guess it's just being in a strange bed.' Even as I said it, I knew I was chained to something beyond my control. It was difficult for me to relax and to trust or give myself completely to anyone, even my husband – or even God. A portion of my energy seemed permanently earmarked for protecting myself. I was afraid that if people knew what had happened, they would not want me or love me.

Opening day came and went. That night my exhausted husband fell asleep immediately, and two nights of not sleeping caught up with me. In my dreams, twenty years dissolved.

I was eleven years old. It was during hunting season, a time filled with the same noises and smells as now. I was sleeping on a cot in my aunt's house. It was a peaceful scene for a short moment. Then suddenly the room filled with swollen blue monsters circling the cot, many monsters, but each wore the same face: the face of one uncle. Each smelled of alcohol. Each wanted to touch me, hurt me.

When I shook myself awake, Ken was holding me, whispering that I was safe. I sat up, trembling, still sensing danger. My chest heaved as if I'd been wrestling. I felt cold and sweaty.

'I want to go home,' I said, pulling away and rubbing at the tears on my cheeks. 'I want to go home right now.'

He smoothed my hair. 'Now? You aren't serious.'

'I'm leaving, Ken.'

'I don't understand.' He looked at me and noticed my quivering hands. His grip on my shoulders tightened.

'Honey? Did you have a nightmare?'

I kept looking down. 'I did.'

'So tell me about it. Just talk about it; then it can't hurt you. It's over.'

'There's nothing to tell you. I just want to leave. If you want to stay, you go ahead, but I'm leaving!' I threw the covers off, went to the wardrobe and pulled my suitcase out. In minutes I had stuffed my things into it and changed into a sweater for the drive home. Ken sat in bed watching in disbelief. I tossed the suitcase on to the covers beside him and glared. 'Well, are you staying or leaving?'

He shook his head. 'This is insane. What are we going to tell your family? We can't just disappear.'

I leaned closer. 'I don't care what we tell them. I don't have to explain myself to anyone!'

Why did I ever agree to this? I thought. What made me think I could come back here? Ken knows something's wrong, God help me!

I couldn't tell him, I couldn't talk about something that might destroy me and everything that mattered in my life.

Now it was almost as if the secret had come out of its corner and was circling my feet, rubbing against me, threatening my sanity even as my husband looked at me with love and concern.

'Not anyone? Not me? Is this something you won't even talk to me about?' He sounded so hurt.

'There's no point in talking about this. It's old, it's past. Talking won't help. I just want to leave.'

'It won't go away,' he said, climbing out of bed. 'If it's this upsetting, it isn't going to vanish when we drive south.' He reached for his shirt.

I wrote my mother a vague note about not feeling well, and then we left. But as we travelled farther and farther from that place, my memory didn't slither back to its assigned spot in the shadows. It stood in the early hints of dawning light that streaked the sky over the pine trees, taunting me.

Ken glanced at me from time to time. I leaned my head against the window, and tears started down my face. The memory seemed almost real ...

I saw my uncle's face. I felt his hands on me. I felt the brush of his red hunting coat. The cot in my memory toppled over and I was pinned to the tile floor. I felt the terror of not understanding what was happening or how an uncle I'd adored could do this to me. I smelled his alcohol-breath. Helpless to stop the scene in my mind, I watched as my uncle raped my childhood and left me crying in the dark on the morning of opening day.

When Ken pulled off the road, it was a shattered child he held and comforted. The flashback left me drained. I shut my eyes and rested in Ken's arms. Clinging together, we sat, silent for a long time. I had not told the secret yet, but it seemed to dare me to tell. I knew I could submerge it again. That would make it okay for a while, but I also knew it would be back. It would remain my master.

Ken kissed my wet cheeks. He looked confused, scared. 'Honey, if you don't talk about this, it's going to eat you up inside. It will be a wall between us. You need to tell someone. If you can't tell me, we'll find someone you can tell. I wish it could be me.'

If ever a person said all the right things at just the right time, it was my husband at that critical moment. So there at the side of the road, I told the secret.

It didn't destroy me, or my marriage. When I finished, Ken cried too, and in his eyes I saw acceptance.

All those years I had been afraid that no one who knew my secret could ever truly love me, not even God. Now that it was out, I felt more loved than I had ever thought I could be.

As Ken pulled back on to the road, the sun was just coming up over the hills to the southeast, pushing back the shadows around the tall pines and flooding the snow-covered landscape with light. It was one of the most glorious sights I had ever seen. It was almost as if God Himself was telling me, 'The secret's power over you is broken.'

And so it was. My healing had begun.

KEEPING A PROMISE

by Sam Stoneburner

No warning could have prepared me for the shock of finding my brother as motionless as a statue.

When I left for the theatre that afternoon, my brother Don was still in his pyjamas, sitting quietly in his favourite chair, staring out of the living room window at the buildings across the street. I told him I'd see him after my performance. He didn't say anything. When I returned home about eight hours later, Don was still in his pyjamas, still in the same position in the same chair, still staring out the window into the dark Manhattan night.

'Don,' I said.

No answer. I shook him gently.

'Don.' No response.

I phoned his psychiatrist immediately. Don had been under treatment for some time, and I'd been warned about this frightening possibility. It's called catatonia, an impenetrable stupor that is the pit of schizophrenia. But no warning could have prepared me for the shock of finding my younger brother as motionless as a marble statue.

His psychiatrist was out. I managed to get Don dressed, then to the street and into a cab. We headed for the nearest hospital. At the emergency room a nurse scanned Don's face, told me to wait, and hurried him to a doctor. When she returned thirty minutes later, her hand was around Don's shoulders, guiding his halting steps.

'He's been sedated,' she explained. 'The doctor says to get him to his psychiatrist as soon as you can.'

'Thank you,' I said. When we got in the cab to return home, Don limply rested his head on my shoulder. This was not our first trip to the hospital.

The earliest indication of Don's illness appeared mysteriously, about ten years before that frightening night. He had spent a long weekend with me during a break in his year at university. We'd always had a lively relationship, but at dinner in a bustling restaurant that first night, Don barely spoke. We went back to my flat and he didn't leave it for the rest of the visit. He was edgy and moody, and I was worried. Then, packing listlessly for the trip back, Don suddenly started sobbing.

'Sam, what's wrong with me?' he pleaded. 'I feel confused and scared. Sometimes I don't know where I am.'

'You're going to be all right,' I said, embracing him. 'We'll find out what's wrong and get it fixed before you return to university.'

Sadly, Don never returned to the university. The psychiatrist who diagnosed his schizophrenia explained, 'The disease often attacks suddenly in early adulthood. There's no known cure. Medication and therapy might stabilize him, but schizophrenia is unpredictable.' He might lapse into depression or suffer terrifying hallucinations. Or, with no warning, Don might sink into a catatonic state and never emerge,' the doctor told me. 'He may be better off in an institution,' he conluded. At the time, I was taking the first rocky steps in my career as an actor, and had to be ready to work anywhere in the country. That meant I could not always be with Don. Still, I had an old promise to keep, and it did not include putting my brother in an institution.

You see, before Don was born I had another brother named Maurice, fourteen months my junior. Our parents were happy to see us grow as close as two sides of a coin. Maurice was seven when he died of a ruptured appendix. In time the tears passed, but the aching loneliness for my brother never quite left. Then one day my mother startled me with an announcement: 'Sam, you're going to have a new brother or sister. But remember, your father and I won't always be here. Someday there will just be the two of you, and you'll have to look after each other. Promise me you'll take care of our new baby. God will help you.'

I told her I would. 'This baby will be my best friend,' I promised. He was named Don, and mother added the name Anthony, after St Anthony, whom Catholics associate with finding lost things. Her prayers to God for another child had been answered, not to replace the child she'd lost but a child to receive the love that was still waiting to be given.

Don was a gentle child, with a curious mind, a love for drawing pictures and, as he grew older, a taste for solo adventures. Before one Christmas, when he was seventeen, he borrowed enough from Dad to rent a piece of land and stock it with Christmas trees. He sold them all, paid back the loan and used the profits for a trip across Europe the following summer.

I was proud of him. His future looked bright when he entered university as an art student. Then came that trip to New York in his final year. From the start of his illness Don was determined to help himself. He was an in-patient and an outpatient at the clinic. I tried to convince him to live with me, but he insisted on being on his own. He rented a room and tried desperately to fit into the real world. He worked in a warehouse, in a library for the blind, and at a gas station. He regularly attended Mass, something I'd stopped doing a long time before. But for Don, church was an anchor in stormy waters.

One morning I picked up Don to take him to breakfast before a rehearsal I had. Afterwards, on the way back to his flat, he suddenly stopped in front of a church. I wanted to remind him that I didn't have much time, but he quickly took my arm and led me inside. The church was cool and peaceful. I slipped into a back pew and remained, in uneasy silence while Don went to the altar rail, lit a candle and knelt in prayer. I stared at the marble floor. I couldn't remember the last time I'd prayed.

Don fought his troubles, but then came the morning I found him sitting in the corner of his room, unshaven and dishevelled. The floor was littered with newspapers and dirty clothes. I got him cleaned up, dressed and fed. The next morning I moved him into my apartment. For a while he seemed to respond to treatment. However, the doctor had warned that the worst could happen at any time. It did, that terrifying night I returned from the theatre to find Don frozen in a catatonic stupor. He was in and out of the hospital after that, and it took a long time to stabilize him. On good days he would draw or paint, and attend Mass every Friday and Sunday. On bad days he retreated behind a wall of silence and gloom. When he emerged, he always prayed aloud while washing his hands or dressing.

The day all actors dream about finally came when I landed a role in a musical: *Six Degrees of Separation*. Don was overjoyed. One cold Sunday morning he shook me awake. 'Sam, please come to Mass with me,' he pleaded. 'Don, I did two shows yesterday,' I protested. 'If I don't get some rest I'll sleepwalk through today's matinee.'

Then I looked out at him from under the covers. The hurt in his eyes made me hop out of bed. 'Okay, Don, wait till I get dressed.' His smile warmed the room.

Before Mass began, Don knelt for his private prayers. Impulsively, I knelt too and whispered, 'Lord, free my brother from his turmoil.' Not much of a prayer, but I was out of practice. As Mass progressed I found myself participating, and remembering more about my faith than I realized I'd lost.

Working in town, I could be with Don on my days off from the show – and during most of the day four times a week. When I had to be away for any length of time, a trusted friend, Kenneth Bennett, would move into my apartment and look after him. Eventually one of my brother's doctors suggested Don might do better away from the frenetic pace of city life. About this time our aunt Virginia became unable to live alone. I bought a house in the suburbs, half an hour or so away, and moved them all in – Kenny, Don and Aunt Virginia. The house was near a mental health clinic, so Don could continue to be seen by specialists.

When Clorazil, a promising new drug for treating schizophrenia, became available, Don's doctor explained that it had to be taken at precise intervals, and it would be best if Don moved to a supervised environment. Don went to a local residence home. He now attends the clinic four days a week, from 10.00 a.m to 3.00 p.m., and then he walks five streets back to the residence home. He's with Aunt Virginia and Kenny from Friday until Sunday. I pop down to see them whenever I can.

One weekend I found Don at the house busily designing a greeting card; on the floor lay a drawing of a bird in flight and a woodcut of a forest scene. I remembered the prayer I'd said the Sunday morning when Don hauled me out of bed for Mass, and the many prayers I have said since. It was not too long ago that Don rarely completed anything he started. God had indeed made him freer of his turmoil.

In church that Sunday I followed Don to the altar rail. We each lit a candle. I don't know what Don's was for, but he says he often lights a candle for me. Mine was for St Anthony, and in thanks to God for helping my brother find some of the peace he lost when a cruel disease struck him down in the full stride of youth.

As I knelt, a thought flashed through my mind: Don was now fifty-three, and for thirty years he had helped me as much as I had helped him. Most of all he had helped me find a lost faith. Isn't that what my mother had said? 'Someday you'll have to look out for each other.' And so we have.

NIGHT OF THE STORM

by Stuart Reininger

'Dad, it's you who won't listen!'

Karin and I stood along the sea wall at the French coastal town of St-Gilles-sur-Vie, gazing out on the Bay of Biscay. As we watched the heaving waves throw spumes of white froth high into the moody grey sky, Karin sighed. 'Doesn't look good, Dad,' she said.

Another day lost, I thought. I'd contracted to deliver a 42-foot sail boat to Florida, and each day of delay was costly. It was mid-November, and the longer Karin and I waited the more likely we were to encounter heavy seas on the Atlantic, slowing our crossing even more.

I glanced at my daughter. Ringlets of her long blonde hair were plastered to her forehead by the briny mist, making her look younger than her twenty-two years. The weather wasn't the only stormy thing of the past week. Karin and I had had our differences, as we so often did. Since her graduation from high school back in New Jersey, Karin had been travelling in Europe, and now, every night in France, we'd had the same argument.

'Why can't you come home and start college?' I would demand. 'Haven't you had enough adventure?'

'Is that why you invited me to sail with you?' she would counter. 'So you could harangue me? You act like you don't trust me!'

'Why won't you listen to me?'

'Dad, it's you who don't listen!'

I had thought this trip would be a chance for me to talk some sense into my daughter. My work as a yacht captain had frequently kept me away from home while Karin was growing up. This, coupled with the anger she still harboured towards me over my divorce from her mother, had driven a wedge between us. I'd prayed that the voyage would bring us closer and help Karin see that I knew what was best for her.

We left the sea wall and headed back to the boat slip to ponder our options. The Bay of Biscay is notorious for its violent storms. Boats caught in bad weather far out to sea rarely get into serious trouble, but in the confines of a bay, even one as large as Biscay, a vessel can be driven on to the rocks in no time. We would have to sail about three hundred miles to clear the bay – three days directly into the prevailing westerly winds – before we could swing south into calmer waters, then west again for home. While the weather wasn't getting any better, it wasn't getting any worse, either. 'Let's go for it,' I told Karin that night.

We sailed at dawn's first light, into a slashing, wind-driven rain. Karin's gaze swept the flinty horizon as I stood at the helm. Maybe by the time we hit open sea some of the chill that had fallen over us would fade. The boat, designed for heavy weather, made good time. The next day we were halfway out of the bay, but the sky blackened, the wind cried and then roared, and by afternoon the growing seas began tossing the boat. I glanced at my daughter. Her features were set in a mask of determination. Whatever our differences, Karin was a top-notch sailor.

Darkness fell early as the boat twisted down steepening waves, slamming from one crest to another. Churning white water crashed over the deck. An ominous sloshing came from the bilge below and the pumps laboured continuously. Karin and I took turns fighting the wheel, and tried to fend off exhaustion. Had we been in open sea I would have turned and run from the storm. Still trapped in the bay, there was little room to manoeuvre; it was a matter of hours before we would be driven towards the rocks, and heading back to St-Gilles was too risky – the channel into the harbour was best negotiated by daylight, in calm waters. There was only one option: to heave to.

This meant taking down the sails and turning into the wind, leaving only one small sail up to keep the boat steady. Karin and I could then go below and get the rest we so desperately needed. The boat would still drift, but much more slowly.

Struggling to be heard above the wind, I shouted to Karin what I planned to do. She nodded her agreement and took the helm as I went to work. As soon as I had finished, the movement of the boat eased and we were able to go below. While going down the hatch Karin put her hand on my arm and smiled, 'It's been a long day,' she said, 'get some sleep, Dad.'

I prayed as I drifted off. Lord, let me make the right decisions, and help me to protect my daughter.

A few hours later, I was jerked awake from a light sleep and thrown from my bunk by the sudden violent motion of the boat being rolled on its side. A gigantic wave slammed into us. Water rushed into the cabin from overhead vents. In the murky darkness Karin's face was sickly pale as she scrambled from her bunk.

'What happened?' she cried.

'A freak wave!' I said, trying to get my balance. It was no use. The boat wasn't righting itself. The roar of the gale had reached a demonic crescendo. I struggled into my jacket and safety harness, and then wedged myself through the hatch and into the cockpit. Karin followed.

The sea towered above the mast like rolling mountains of water. In all my years of sailing, I had not seen anything like it. The wind was so strong that the small sail I had left up was pinning the boat on its side. We'd capsize if another wave struck us in this prone position.

I thought that if I could get the sail down, we might be able to turn the boat and run ahead of the wind. That would take us back towards the treacherous shoreline; it would also buy us some time.

'I'm going to get that sail down!' I shouted.

Attaching my harness line to the cockpit, I levered myself on to the cabin and inched towards the mast. I was only a few feet out when the wind sent me hurtling back into the cockpit. I glanced at Karin, hoping she couldn't detect panic on my face. 'What if we ease it?' she shouted. 'We'd be able to steer then.'

She was right. The line that controlled the sail led to the cockpit. It would be risky to try to ease the sail out in this wind; the mast might snap. If it worked, though, we would be able to turn the boat away from the wind. We'd be running even faster to the shore, but we had no choice.

'Okay!' I hollered, grasping for the cleat that held the sail line. I pulled with all my might. It was jammed! Karin and I struggled with the line. There was no freeing it. Any second now another huge wave might complete the job which the first one had just barely failed to do.

I whipped out my pocket knife and shouted, 'I'm cutting the line!' Once loose, the sail would be torn to shreds. Most likely, the mast would snap. The boat would finally right itself, and we'd be at the mercy of the wind; our only hope of survival would be the gale blowing itself out before we were dashed against the rocks.

I laid the blade beside the taut, twisted rope. It was a desperate move. Just then I felt Karin's hand on my arm.

'Don't do it, Dad!'

I looked at her in disbelief. 'Don't cut it. Something tells me the storm will ease soon. I've been timing the waves. They're not hitting as often.' The night was pitch-black. The boat was still pinned on its side. The wind and sea hadn't let up. All my instincts screamed, cut the line!

'Please, Dad. Trust me!'

I hesitated. Trust me. Had I ever really trusted anyone but myself? Could I trust Karin? I was always so sure I knew what was best.

I put the knife back in my pocket. 'All right, we'll try it your way,' I said. A surge of relief overtook me.

Karin was right. Within a few hours the wind let up, and by morning the gale had passed and we were on our way. In the weeks it took to get home, Karin and I talked and grew closer, and slowly I saw my daughter as the strong and capable woman she had become.

That crossing was six years ago. Eventually, Karin had her fill of travel and adventure, and started college near home. She graduated last year and teaches at a local school.

My work still involves boats, but I stay close to home port these days. I try to put into practice what I learned that storm-tossed night on the Bay of Biscay. The key to love is faith – and being able to trust those whom we love and who love us.

SOUND SLEEPER

by Virginia Seters

All was still, and yet I felt that I had been awakened for some reason.

I am a sound sleeper. Only thirst or a headache ever wakes me up. I can sleep through almost anything – a car speeding past, a dog barking, a passing thunderstorm. For no apparent reason I woke up with a start one cool, autumn night.

At first I thought it was time to get up. No, my clock showed it was only 1 a.m. in the morning. All was still, and yet I felt that I had been awakened for some reason. I sat bolt upright on the side of the bed. Several minutes passed. The bedroom windows were closed and the curtains were drawn. No noise came from the outside. There was total silence.

Then I distinctly heard a man's voice: 'Help me, help me! Oh, please someone help me!'

Immediately I reached for the telephone and dialled the emergency services. 'Someone needs help,' I said. 'Someone out near my street.' I told the operator where I lived and, satisfied that I had done all I could, I went back to bed.

Even before I fell asleep, a policewoman called me back. She sounded incredulous. 'How did you know someone was there?' she asked.

'I heard his cries,' I answered.

'But how could you?' she asked. She knew my block of flats was set well back from the street. My windows were closed and I hadn't heard the police drive by.

'The man you heard', she explained, 'was trapped in a car at the bottom of a ravine nearly two streets away.'

'I heard him,' I said. Somehow, I had heard him.

SNOW BRIDGE RESCUE

by Jim Smith

As we forged on at forty miles per hour, something disturbing was happening.

Two years ago in March, I was on an excursion with three other businessmen. We were taking our snowmobiles over some of Alaska's wildest and most spectacular terrain. As we sped along a well-worn trail across vast glaciers, I couldn't help being awestruck by the stark beauty of the endless expanse of ice and snow – so breathtaking that it was easy to forget it was also some of Alaska's most dangerous country.

The zero-degree air pinched our nostrils, and crystalline streamers spewed from behind our four snowmobiles. The late winter sun glittered off the snow against a backdrop of hulking mountains. Riding on the lead machine was Bobby Havemeister, who was twenty-seven years old. Following him was Howard Riley, aged thirty-four, and Gary Pinckert, who was thirty-four, was behind him. I was last in the line, and my machine was the one carrying the canvas tent and down sleeping bag. I felt foolish since it was just a day trip, but my wife, Garnet, had insisted I take the stuff.

'I know you think I'm off the wall, Jim,' she said, 'but I have this feeling you might need it.'

To Garnet this was just common sense, but in view of what happened, my three friends say it was the hand of God. All had a deep faith that buttressed their daily lives. They were always trying to get me to go to church. But I just wasn't comfortable with that kind of hands-on religion.

As we reached high country, our trail began threading across a series of glaciers, some more than thirty miles long. These huge ice masses, hundreds of feet deep, move down the mountains almost imperceptibly. There can be peril in crossing them, because hidden under snow bridges are deep, plunging crevasses. When a bridge is weak and gives way, unwary trekkers can plummet without warning into fathomless fissures, never to be found.

When you are born here, as I was, you develop a sixth sense about these fragile bridges. Our trail had been blazed by the Motor Mushers, a group of experienced locals who carefully search out safe trails across these glaciers and deep-groove them with their machines.

As we forged on at forty-five miles per hour, something disturbing was happening. It was getting difficult to see anything, yet it wasn't dark. We were in a white-out, a vision-distorting phenomenon in which there is almost no depth perception. A glacier is a perilous place to lose your bearings.

I intensified my concentration, to no avail. Soon I lost the horizon and all points of reference. Worse, my Polaris, slower than the others, kept falling behind. Only intermittently could I catch the red glow of tail lights. The light grew stranger, and I found myself in an alien world. Even the howl of the engines up ahead was deceptive. Suddenly I couldn't hear them at all. A feeling of dread crept up my spine. Could they have swerved off the trail? Something's not right, I kept thinking.

Spooked, I throttled down to thirty miles per hour, then twenty-five, then slower, wondering what was wrong. I strained to see. And then, a strange command flashed into my mind – urgent, imperative. There was no mistaking it. *Jump!*

Without a thought, I flung myself from the machine, and it continued speeding into the eerie whiteness. I struggled to my feet in a daze and was astonished to find myself at the rim of a snow bowl measuring about 150 feet across and some six stories deep. I peered down to the bottom to see my Polaris, its track still spinning, crashed on top of Howard's machine. Howard seemed okay – he was standing there, staring up at me. He pointed urgently to Bobby, who was hunched in the snow, and called to me, 'Bobby's shoulder's broken.

A machine fell on him. And Gary's in real bad shape.' He motioned to a ten-foot-deep pit in the bottom of the snow bowl. In its shadowy depths sprawled Gary, lying unconscious next to his wrecked snowmobile.

I slid down into the bowl and my sixth sense immediately told me that the whole area was riddled with hidden crevasses. Worse than this, the pit in which Gary lay was likely a snow bridge itself, the only thing between him and oblivion.

I quickly learned that Bobby, who had been in the lead, had been disoriented by the white-out, had veered off the trail and plunged over the lip of the snow bowl. Howard and Gary had unwittingly followed him. Gary's machine flipped in mid-air before careering off the side of the bowl and into the deep pit.

As I stared helplessly at Gary, Howard frantically tried to start Bobby's snowmobile, which, despite bent steering gear, appeared operable. Finally it roared to life. 'I'm going to get help!' he yelled. He gunned up the bowl's steep slope only to slide back again and again. Finally, in a blast of snow, he was over the top and heading for Valdez, a good two hours away.

I slogged over to the pit and worked my way down to Gary. He was in agony and slipping into shock; his eyes were closed and his clammy skin had a deathly pallor. His helmet lay some distance away, and I worried about a head injury. I needed to keep him warm. But two of us on that snow bridge along with a 600-pound machine? I shuddered. There was no way of knowing the thickness of the bridge, or how deep the chasm below was.

Gary groaned. I glanced anxiously at my Polaris, where the sleeping bag and tent were rolled up on the carrier. There was only one thing to do. I retrieved the sleeping bag and tent and climbed back down to Gary. I spread the tent on to the snow underneath him and worked the bag up around his shoulders. 'I ... am so cold,' he moaned. The sleeping bag wasn't doing the job.

'I'm going to crawl in beside you,' I told Gary. 'Don't move.' Then I wriggled my five-foot-ten-inch frame into the one-man sleeping bag, hoping the snow bridge would hold. Bitter cold sucked the heat from our bodies, and I pulled my coat over our heads. Then Bobby, grimacing with pain, hobbled down and gingerly zipped us up. As the warmth in the down bag began to build, Gary's moaning stopped. He opened his eyes.

'How did I get here?' he asked.

'Don't worry about it, buddy,' I assured him. 'Help is on the way.'

But when? Will Howard make it? What if his battered snowmobile gives out? And underlying all my thoughts was the ominous sense that only a thin arch of snow supported us.

An hour went by. Bobby huddled by his snowmobile. I kept assuring Gary again and again, 'Help is coming, old buddy.' Another hour passed and long blue shadows crept across the snow.

'God,' I suddenly found myself pleading, 'I don't know where you are, if you are, but please get us out of here.' I thought about my belief in my capacity to overcome adversity on my own, my pride in my strength alone. 'God, I'm doing all I can but it's not good enough. Please take over.'

Then Bobby said, 'If they send a helicopter, we need something a pilot can zero in on.' All he came up with was a small red gas can. He positioned it on the rim of the bowl. Will it be visible? I wondered.

'I ... I'm thirsty,' Gary moaned. I reached around and found the water bottle. He gulped the liquid. I closed my eyes. Please, God, please.

Then Bobby lifted his head, 'I hear something!' I rose on one elbow. Yes, there it was – the muffled chop of a helicopter. Soon it skimmed over us and landed. Two men jumped out and I climbed up to help them. 'Couldn't have found you if it hadn't been for that red gas can,' one of them said. Wary of the danger, they used waist ropes as one carefully walked down to Gary.

'You're very lucky,' he said, shaking his head. After lifting Gary on to a litter, they carried him into the helicopter and flew him to the hospital in Valdez, then rushed back for Bobby and me. Reaching Valdez was a miracle in itself. In the eerie half-light, the helicopter bounced and yawed as the pilot fought winds while at the same time negotiating the mountainous terrain. Finally we made it to the hospital. We learned that Gary's multiple injuries included a shattered pelvis, but that he would pull through.

An exhausted Howard told us of his struggle to get help. 'I couldn't see more than a yard ahead of me,' he said. 'I had to hop off my snowmobile to test for crevasses almost every foot of the way. I don't know how I made it.'

When Howard finally reached Valdez, he ran smack into yet another miracle. The fire department had assembled for its yearly helicopter safety briefing.

'I could hardly believe it,' he said. 'Trained rescue workers were all set to go!'

They didn't have a minute to spare. The doctors said that Gary's vital signs had all but disappeared by the time he arrived in Valdez. He couldn't have survived much longer.

Gary and Bobby recovered, and all four of us – yes, that's right, all four – are convinced that God saved us. For I know now that something far stronger than luck was supporting that snow bridge. And today I also know that something far more powerful and ever-present than my own strength supports my life.

TEN MINUTES OF TERROR

by Don Clendenin

An underlying fear had crept into my daily life.

Returning from a quick errand to the DIY shop, I slipped the key into the front door of my home. My wife Pam was still out shopping. A queasy sense of apprehension filled me, a feeling that had become so familiar lately. I let myself in and flipped on a couple of overhead lights, though it was still daylight. Come on, Don, I admonished myself. You're acting crazy.

I couldn't help it. After putting down my package, I climbed the stairs and walked to the bedroom. Crouching, I glanced under the bed. Then I checked the wardrobes, the bathroom and the back stairs until I'd convinced myself that there was no one waiting to leap out at me. It had become an unnerving routine, ever since the day, a couple of months earlier, when I had been a victim of a savage attack. At the time everyone called me brave, but an underlying fear had crept into my daily life. I sat down exhausted at the kitchen table, and let my mind roll back to December 1991.

I was running late that chilly morning, so I'd skipped breakfast. We were busy with Christmas orders at Bernhardt Furniture, where I'm the shipping manager. Just before noon I remembered that I had told Pam I would take Brownie, our Chow-Samoyed mix, to Pet Fashions for a 12.15 grooming appointment.

I raced home to pick him up, not stopping for lunch. Then I headed for the grooming parlour. I had never been there before, but I had the address tucked in the back of my mind. It looked like I'd be right on time, so I relaxed. Our town is mostly full of good, hard-working people, but recently we've had our share of drug problems and crime. Still, I tried to maintain a basic trust in people.

Pet Fashions was in a modest, semi-detached house. The tiny reception area was empty, but off to the left was a room with dogs in cages; they exchanged yaps with Brownie. I couldn't see into the other room. I was about to turn the corner to go in when I heard scuffling and then a terrified scream.

I dropped Brownie's leash and burst in. A large man was pinning a young woman to the floor and stabbing her with scissors. Blood poured from the wounds to her face. I grabbed the man's arm and tried to throw him off the woman, shouting, 'Stop! Let her go!' He leapt to his feet and came at me. He lunged, shoving me hard; I fell back and crashed against the wall. Then he was on me, jabbing with the scissors. The woman pulled herself up, staggered into a bathroom and slammed the door. As the attacker and I struggled, we fell back into the reception area. I heard dogs barking in the background as we grappled.

The scissors plunged into the side of my neck. He stabbed me again. I kept fighting him, finally getting a grip on the blades. I jerked them out of his hand, then braced my feet against his stomach and pushed with all my might. He fell backwards and away from me. I got to my feet and stared at the blood-smeared scissors in my hand. Maybe he'll leave now I thought, but when I looked up he was coming at me again. He was an imposing figure and he had a crazy look in his glazed eyes. I tried to stay calm. In that instant a prayer, flashed into my mind: Please, God, help me.

He came on slowly. As I backed away, the words jumped out of my mouth: 'Get out! Leave right now!' I kept my eyes level with his, afraid even to blink, and edged my hand towards the doorknob and turned it slowly. 'No one will stop you.' He glanced at the escape route as I took a deep breath and stepped back. 'Just get out.'

He looked at me, then to my amazement, turned and ran. I slammed the door shut and dashed over to the bathroom. 'He's gone!' I called to the woman inside.

'Oh, thank God you came,' she gasped, stumbling out. 'He would have killed me. He was trying to rob the shop.'

I called the police, blurted out the address, and soon an ambulance rushed us to the hospital, where we both underwent surgery. In the recovery room I found out the woman, 22-year-old Carolyn Young, was all right. I felt relieved, even though the police had not yet found the man who had attacked us.

The next afternoon when Pam left my hospital room for a few minutes, I closed my eyes for a nap. I was just beginning to doze, when suddenly the nightmarish scene replayed itself. Scissors were plunging at me again, and I saw those awful, glowering eyes. I awoke with a terrible jolt. For an instant it had felt as if I were right back at the grooming parlour, fighting for my life. Then that night, while I was in the bathroom, I thought I heard a strange noise outside the door. My heart began to race. He's come to the hospital to finish the job. I don't know how long I stayed in the bathroom until I convinced myself it was safe to come out.

I was discharged after a few days, and within the week the police arrested the attacker. I thought my fears would subside, now that I knew that he was behind bars. Instead, I found myself watching strangers, and jumping whenever someone walked up behind me. I had been a trusting man, but suddenly I didn't feel like I could trust anyone. Crime wasn't just something that I read about in the newspapers; it had happened to me. I no longer felt safe in my own home, even after a short trip to the DIY shop. Now, sitting at the kitchen table in my quiet, empty house, I asked God if I would ever regain my sense of security.

When I phoned Carolyn it relieved me somewhat to learn that she was going through the same fears. We talked several times, seeing if we could ease our apprehension. But still I found myself checking the wardrobes and peering under the bed.

One night after dinner Pam and I discussed the attack again. I felt that the more I could talk about that day the better I'd eventually feel. Pam patted my shoulder.

'I think being afraid after what you've gone through is only natural, but it's got to the point where an event that lasted ten minutes is affecting your whole life. Some terrible things happened in those minutes, but now it's time to think positively about them.'

Pam was right. If she hadn't asked me to take Brownie to be

groomed, the pet shop would have been the last place in the world I'd have been that day, and Carolyn might have been killed. If I hadn't taken the 12.15 appointment, Carolyn would have given it to an older lady who'd called right after me. God had certainly been with me when I told the attacker to get out of the shop. Incredibly, the man left. If he were going to 'finish the job' he would have done so then. The police later discovered that he had been carrying a large carving knife when he first came in.

God's touch was also evident in such simple things as my not having had time to eat breakfast or lunch. If I had eaten, doctors said, surgery could have been much harder on me. A surgeon told me that one of my wounds had missed my jugular vein by one quarter of an inch.

Even in the fear and confusion of the moment I was able quickly to give the emergency operator the address I had come to for the first time ever.

When Pam and I finished, there was no doubt in our minds that lives had been saved because things had happened exactly the way they had. We were amazed at how much we had to be thankful to God for. He had threaded me through the eye of a needle.

Pam washed the dishes while I went up to our room. As I sat on the edge of the bed untying my shoes, I thought, Okay, Lord, the next time I get down on my knees to check under this bed, I'm going to say a prayer to you to help me feel safe again. I want to trust you in all things.

The following months were difficult. It's strange, but regaining trust was harder than fighting off the attacker. Eventually I healed, inside and out, and even took Brownie back to Carolyn for his grooming. I'm a more cautious person these days, naturally, but I'm learning to trust again too.

VOYAGE OF HOPE

by Thomas Fleming

The shock of the ninety-mile-an-hour impact was terrific.

'Do you mind if I pray?' asked navigator Johnny DeAngelis as the plane began to fall into the ocean.

Co-pilot Jim Whittaker almost told him to shut up. Prayer was synonymous with weakness as far as he was concerned. Only brains and nerve were going to get them out of this mess.

'Five feet!' Eddie Rickenbacker barked in Whittaker's ear. 'Three feet ... One foot. Cut it!'

Whittaker pulled the mainline switch, knocking out all the electrical connections in the hurtling Army Air Corps B-17 Flying Fortress. Pilot Bill Cherry pancaked the big plane in the exact centre of a trough between two huge Pacific swells.

The shock of the ninety-mile-an-hour impact was terrific. Whittaker thought his seat belt would slice him in two. But the five-man crew and their three passengers managed to scramble out of the sinking plane with only minor injuries. Inflating three yellow rafts, they tied them together with a long towline.

They had no idea where they were. The plane's navigational equipment had failed as they flew southwest from Hawaii, and they had tried to determine their location until they ran out of fuel. The nearest land might be more than one thousand miles away. Their only hope was that an air-sea search by the US Navy would respond to the SOS radioman Jimmy Reynolds had repeatedly flashed as they ditched.

The ditching had occurred at 4.30 p.m. on 21 October 1942, ten and a half months after the Japanese attack on Pearl Harbour. Two of the passengers were Eddie Rickenbacker and his friend Colonel Hans Adamson, who were on their way to the South Pacific to inspect American airfields. The third passenger, Sergeant Alex Kaczmarczyk, was returning to his regiment after a seven-week bout of jaundice.

They had no water; their only food was four oranges. Their only equipment was two sets of oars, some sheath knives, a few fishhooks and some line that one of them had snatched from a parachute kit before he jumped from the plane.

During the night the soaked men shivered in the tiny rafts, which seemed to maintain five inches of water in their bottoms no matter how much they bailed. In the morning the tropic sun rose. All around them they saw the dorsal fins of circling sharks.

Their hopes plunged as the day passed with no sign of a search plane. By nightfall they were in an agony of thirst. The second day was more of the same. Towards the end of that day, Whittaker noticed the plane's engineer, red-haired Johnny Bartek, was reading a khaki-covered New Testament he had taken from his pocket. On the fourth day they were down to their last orange. Their hunger was agonizing. They began talking about cutting off fingers or toes to use as bait on their fishhooks. Suddenly a sea swallow, a bird about half the size of a seagull, landed on Eddie Rickenbacker's head. Within seconds it was seized and its raw flesh distributed among the rafts. They used the bird's intestines as bait and quickly caught several small fish, which they sliced up and shared in the same way.

This did not solve their water problem. If anything, the raw fish intensified their thirst. Johnny Bartek wondered if they ought to have a prayer meeting. Whittaker had no enthusiasm for the idea. But Rickenbacker, a man who had survived countless aerial combats and a harrowing commercial plane crash, agreed. They pulled the rafts together and Colonel Adamson, as the senior officer, was asked to read from Bartek's Bible. He read from Matthew, the sixth chapter, 'So do not start worrying: where will my food come from? Or my drink? Or my clothes? Your father in heaven knows that you need all these things.'

Jim Whittaker remarked that he had been exposed to Bible teaching as a boy in Missouri, but for most of his life he had been disdainful of religion. He felt God had never done much for him, so why should he worship? After another miserable night in the rafts, Whittaker dismissed the verses from Matthew with the bitter thought that he would believe them when he saw some food and drink.

They began and ended the sixth day with prayer services and more readings from Bartek's New Testament. Whittaker, now almost mad from hunger and thirst, could barely restrain his contempt. Afterwards Cherry performed another evening ritual: he fired a flare from a pistol into the darkening sky, hoping it would attract a search plane. Several of the flares had been duds. This one also malfunctioned and fell back into the sea, where it zigzagged around them, burning brightly. A school of good-sized fish were attracted by the light and attacked by barracuda. Two of the hunted fish leapt out of the water and landed in Whittaker's raft. They were quickly killed and sliced up for distribution.

All right, Whittaker told himself. God – or luck – had sent them food. But it was lack of water that was going to kill them long before they starved to death.

On the eighth evening, they wallowed into another choppy, chilling twilight, and Whittaker noticed a cloud on their left beginning to change from fleecy white to darkish blue. A curtain of rain descended on the sea and began moving towards them.

'Thank you, Lord!' Bill Cherry cried as the squall deluged them with sheets of cold, drinkable water. They caught the rain in their hands and poured it down their parched throats. They held up their shirts and wrung water from them into their Mae West life jackets, to build up a reserve.

Whittaker worked at saving the water as frantically as the rest of them, while within his soul a spiritual earthquake took place. God had answered Cherry's prayers. Was it time for Whittaker to start praying too? The next morning the sun scorched them again. As the ninth and tenth days passed with no rescuers, one man begged God to kill him. Rickenbacker took charge. 'Cut that out!' he roared. 'Don't bother him with that whining! He answers men's prayers.'

When Rickenbacker prayed, he asked God to do specific things:

to guide the rescuers to them, to help them reach land. Once he added: 'You, our Father, know we are not asking you to do it all. We will help ourselves, if you will give us a chance.'

On the eleventh day another cloud darkened and spilled rain on them. Again they gulped the water as it came down, and frantically tried to save some of it. As the squall intensified, it tipped over the smallest raft in which Sergeant Kaczmarczyk was riding. When the men got him into one of the bigger rafts, they realized he was dying. He had never uttered a word of complaint throughout the ordeal. He died the next night and they recited prayers for his soul and released his body to the depths.

On the thirteenth day the sun still scorched them. Rain began falling about a mile away, but the wind veered and it moved away from them. 'God,' Jim Whittaker prayed aloud, 'you know what that water means to us. It is in your power to send back that rain.' Some men scoffed at this plea. Whittaker himself was amazed by the words that had leapt from his lips. But he accepted them, confessing the birth of faith in his proud, lonely soul. The bluish-black curtain of water began moving towards them – against the wind! Within minutes, it was drenching the rafts.

On the morning of the fourteenth day the wind died completely. They were in the doldrums. By this time, everyone's lower body was a mass of saltwater ulcers. Their clothing had disintegrated and the sun began to inflict serious burns on them. The water had also rotted the fishing lines and the sharks had snapped them off. The men were living on a few sips of water a day.

Only Rickenbacker refused to give up. He berated anyone who said a discouraging word. At the prayer service that ended the fourteenth day, he led them in asking God for wind to blow them out of the doldrums. No wind appeared. Instead, on the eighteenth and nineteenth days came blows that would have destroyed them, if they had not built up their courage with those hours of daily prayer.

At twilight on the eighteenth day, a search plane passed within three miles without sighting them. Rickenbacker insisted that if the plane came once, it could come again. It returned twice – and missed them both times. Some of the men groaned and despaired, but Jim Whittaker did not join them. As he thought of the amazing answers to so many of their prayers, he became convinced that God was not going to abandon them.

On the twentieth day they decided to separate, in order to give the search planes a better chance of spotting them. Although another plane flew close and failed to see them, Whittaker still felt strangely hopeful. The next morning Johnny DeAngelis shook Whittaker awake and pointed toward the horizon, 'It may be a mirage, but I think I see something.'

It was a line of palm trees. Whittaker began rowing towards them. Neither DeAngelis nor Jimmy Reynolds was strong enough to sit up, much less row. Whittaker himself, before he saw those trees, had been so weak he could not have bent a pin. Yet he somehow found the strength to row for seven and a half hours.

Finally the island was only 250 yards away. The palm trees swayed invitingly. With no warning a current seized the raft and swept them a mile offshore.

'God,' Whittaker prayed, 'give me a little more strength.'

He went back to rowing. Rain descended, soaking and invigorating him, but making it hard to find the island.

Then a twelve-foot-long grey form slid under the raft and slashed at an oar. Another shark bumped the raft, trying to upset it.

'God!' cried Whittaker. 'Don't quit on me now.'

Almost instantly he felt strength surge in his arms and shoulders. The rain continued to sluice down in torrents. The sharks continued to attack. But Whittaker rowed past them, oblivious. Ahead lay one more danger: a reef. But swells lifted them over the jagged stone teeth and minutes later, the raft touched land.

Soon friendly natives helped them to their huts and notified the US Navy. They learned search planes had rescued Bill Cherry, Rickenbacker and the others. When Jim Whittaker recovered from his ordeal, he went home to tell his story to defence workers across America.

'I told them how during those blazing days I found my God.' He vowed to tell his story again and again as long as he lived, because it was 'the greatest story a man can tell'.

WRESTLING WITH ALLIGATORS

by Robert Green

Whump! A reptilian head reared up two feet from my face!

I figured my assignment would be routine that night in 1991. Some older folks in a trailer park had called the Florida Game and Fresh Water Fish Commission, worried about a big alligator in a nearby pond. My job as a trapper is to capture and relocate such animals to an area where they won't be a nuisance.

Night is the best time to find these wary critters. They usually lurk underwater with only their eyes protruding. It's possible to spot them because in the dark those eyes reflect light like balls of fire. After kissing my wife and three daughters goodnight, I loaded my gear into the pickup: a coil of heavy rope and a roll of electrician's tape, a miner's headlamp with waist-mounted battery, and a 'bang stick' – a pole rigged to fire a .44-calibre bullet. The stick was in case I had to kill a dangerous animal, but that was the last thing I wanted to do. I firmly believe that God put these creatures, as with all his creation, on earth for a reason.

Believing that we've been given responsibility for the earth's animals, means respecting and taking care of them. I have loved animals all my life, and feel a particular sympathy for alligators. Once killed indiscriminately until they were nearly extinct, alligators are now protected by law. Granted, their looks don't exactly warm your heart, but they are basically solitary creatures who are afraid of humans unless – and here's the trouble – people feed them. It's against the law, but ignorant people will toss them marshmallows, bread, and other snacks. As a result, alligators lose their fear of humans and associate them with food. Sadly, that's when an animal may turn into a menace and have to be destroyed.

This happened to one unfortunate gator who was befriended by secretaries at an electric company in Palm Bay. The women ate lunch each day at an outdoor picnic table and began sharing their sandwiches with him. They thought it cute to find him waiting every noon. They didn't think it so cute, however, when he tried to force his way into their building. Now their lunch partner has been turned into expensive pocketbooks. I prefer a live animal any time.

That's why, when I headed my pickup to Merritt Island that night, I was grateful my quarry wasn't considered dangerous. I'd be able to transport him alive to an uninhabited area. Such places are becoming scarce in Florida. Alligators are being squeezed out by tourism, shopping centres, golf courses and water pollution.

As I drove on I remembered my father teaching me how animals benefit from one another. Years ago, as we walked around our central Florida farm, he had pointed to a big tree loaded with white egrets.

'Know why that place is a good place for a rookery son? Because a big gator lives in that water hole beneath it. He helps protect the birds from the racoons, possums and snakes that prey on them. If that gator leaves, the rookery could be in trouble.'

Dad showed me a water-filled wallow. 'Gator made that for his home,' he said. 'Comes a bit drought, other animals depend on it for drinking, and the gator gets some easy meals he wouldn't get otherwise.' Dad called a lot of these mutually beneficial arrangements nature's balance. 'God's plan for everything interacting.' Scientists call this symbiosis.

Around midnight I pulled up to the pond. The gator wasn't anywhere to be seen, but the water backed up into a wild swampy area. I figured he'd be in there. Stashing my rope, tape and bang stick by a palm tree, I crawled into the thicket looking for signs of him. The air was fetid and humid. My headlamp cast crazy shadows as I crept through the cat-tails, my knees banging on twisted tree roots and my hair snagged by thorny bushes. All of a sudden I spotted his trail.

As I crouched, deciding where to set a trap, I heard a rustle. Then, whump! A reptilian head reared up two feet from my face!

We both froze. He wasn't any happier to see me up close and personal than I was to see him. Lifting his seven-foot-long body on clawed feet, he turned and lunged down the trail towards the water. Not wanting to lose him, I dove on to his armour-plated back, groping for a hold around his neck, but my fingers couldn't meet. His strong, musky smell filled my nostrils. Scaly skin jabbed my stomach as I bear-hugged the writhing creature. He swung his huge head at me, massive jaws snapping with the speed of a rattler. I knew those teeth could tear off my arm in a second.

Now we were into a real wrestling match. I grasped at his jaws. A gator's powerful jaw-closing muscles can crunch iron-hard tortoise shells like a biscuit. But he uses a weaker set of muscles to open his mouth and if you can get a grip around them and keep his mouth closed, you have a chance.

He bucked and twisted, his ferocious growls and hisses vibrating through me as I clung to him. Finally, with my legs wrapped around him, and his head pressed to the ground, he quietened down. Then, as if gaining strength, the gator exploded, twisting wildly. It was all I could do to keep a grip on him as he lunged and jerked.

Suddenly, a swaying myrtle bush knocked over my headlamp, leaving me in total blackness. Holding the gator's mouth closed with my right hand, I frantically rummaged with my left in the weeds to retrieve the lamp. Finally I managed to slip it back on and re-plug the cord into the battery pack. I tried to drag his gyrating body inch by inch across jumbled roots and through thick brush to the tree where I had stashed the tape and rope. But a bush hit the headlamp and again sent it flying into the weeds. As if sensing his opportunity, the animal slammed me with his tail, sending me sprawling.

I had a job to do. I needed to get this gator, and stay alive in the process. I grabbed him again and yanked him along. Five feet. Ten feet. My arms ached, my hands throbbed. Twenty-five feet. Half standing, half kneeling, I dug my boots into the earth and dragged the thrashing alligator another seventy-five feet.

With one last heave I pulled the animal to the palm tree. I groped for the tape with my left hand, pulled off a length with my teeth and wrapped it around the alligator's jaws. Then I roped him to the tree and collapsed on the ground. It was 2.30 a.m., one and a half hours since our battle had begun. He was tired too and spent the night there safely until I went back to collect him in the morning.

I loaded him into the back of my pickup and drove to a secluded area in central Florida. There I eased my friend into knee-deep water where he'd feel safe. After untying him, I removed the tape that bound his jaws and watched him swim into the tea-coloured stream. Like all of us, he deserved the chance to start over again.

I stood surveying the peaceful scene. A snowy egret high-stepped elegantly through the shallows, a pelican swooped past grey-mussed trees, another alligator on a far rock sunned himself like some prehistoric relic, and I remembered God looking at everything that he had made, and saying how good it was. There are those who wrinkle their noses at alligators and ask, 'Just what good are they?' Well, to my way of thinking, God's 'everything' includes alligators.

TRUE CONFESSION

by Paul Galanti

At that instant of spiritual and psychological checkmate, I experienced something so powerful that it still affects my life to this day.

I was lashed to a wooden stool in an unheated interrogation room at what we POWs ruefully called the Hanoi Hilton. The ropes binding my hands behind me cut deep into my wrists. On the floor a few feet in front of me was a bowl of watery gruel in a rusted, lopsided tin. This was day ten of another period of torture and interrogation.

By then I had been a prisoner of the North Vietnamese for two and a half years after being shot down during my ninety-seventh combat mission. After I ejected from my crippled Navy Skyhawk attack bomber, an enemy bullet had caught me in the neck while I dangled helplessly from my parachute. Captured, I had been forced to march for twelve days to the prison in Hanoi. There the process of breaking me down began, as it did for all POWs, with trying to force me to sign a written confession of my 'war crimes'. I was brutally beaten and psychologically tortured. Still, like most of my compatriots, I refused to sign.

I eyed the battered tin, as did the rats in the grimy, freezing room. To eat, I had to rock my stool until it fell forward. Then, like a starving animal, I would lap up my one daily ration of gruel, hoping the guard outside wouldn't wait too long before coming in and pulling me upright again, lest the rats eat the dribbles of food off my chin. But this was a respite. Sooner or later another torture session would begin.

Torture could last hours at a time. They used a rope contraption to twist my limbs into pretzel-like contortions, tightening the restraints until the agony was beyond unbearable and the only reality was the stupefying pain. When my mind drifted, my captors' shouts and slaps penetrated the haze, bringing me back.

Worse in some ways was the time between interrogations. Dragged back to my dingy cell, I languished in cramped isolation for months. I was forbidden to speak with my fellow prisoners, communicating only sporadically by whispering and surreptitious tapping in code on the walls. The days passed mostly in silence. I spent long, solitary hours trying to keep myself sane by formulating to the minutest detail all the grand business schemes I planned to carry out after the war. Sometimes I watched what we called Hanoi racing spiders, big furry things that could actually rout the rats and devour the lizards that sped over the rough, clammy walls.

I couldn't take my eyes off the gruel. I knew I needed its paltry nourishment to endure another round of barbarous punishment in the interrogation room, but I could not bring myself to fall over and lap it up. I tried to pray for strength. *Dear Lord ...*

Even quasi-religious types like me turned to prayer regularly in the Hanoi Hilton. I was the son of a highly decorated Army colonel and had attended ecumenical chapels at bases all over the world for most of my life. But faith had never meant much to me. I was more interested in the hard-living, girl-chasing image that fighter pilots cultivated. I toned that down when I married Phyllis, but religion was still pretty much a Sunday morning kind of thing for me.

On Sunday mornings at the Hanoi Hilton, though, I at last made a deep connection with faith. None of us could afford to turn his back on God. Three deliberate, commanding thumps on the wall were the signal for all of us to stand for services. Alone in our cells, we said the Lord's Prayer, our voices mingling in the narrow passageway outside.

Now, awaiting the return of my tormentors and trying to gather an appetite for the cold slop in the dirty pan, I felt I couldn't go on, even with God's help. I was too weak, too broken. I would never sign a confession, but I couldn't endure much more of this agony. What was the sense of eating? I was dying anyway, dying from the inside out, not just from the pain but also from the utter senselessness of it. I was at a point where it seemed almost a crime to go on living. I decided I wouldn't eat. I would die instead.

Slumped on my stool at that instant of spiritual and psychological checkmate, I experienced something so powerful that it still affects my life to this day. With complete clarity I realized I was not alone in that desolate room. The veil of suffering lifted and I clearly saw a figure standing near me. He wore a white robe more vivid than any earthly garment I have ever seen. Though I could not make out his features, I listened to his voice with my whole being, as he told me, 'Paul, you are going to be all right. I am always with you.'

I was still bound, but suddenly I felt free, the flames of my despair smothered by comfort and reassurance. Those words, I knew, were the words of Jesus, delivered by an angel. It was God alone who had command over life, and He was telling me that with him all suffering could be endured, all pain soothed.

Suddenly my companion was no longer visible, and I was alone again with my pitiful meal. Yet it beckoned me like a feast. I tipped over the stool and ate gratefully.

I survived two more weeks of intermittent torture with the interrogators, and for four more years I was a captive in the Hanoi Hilton. In 1973 I was finally able to come home and get started on some of those business plans I had dreamed up in my prison cell. That day when the angel delivered the words that saved me, I *did* make a confession – a confession of faith. My life was saved, not just once but for ever.

USEFUL ADDRESSES

Reading these stories may encourage you to think about your own struggles. If you would like further help on your life journey, here is a list of agencies that may be able to help:

British Association for Counselling
1 Regent Place
Rugby
Warks CV21 2PJ
01788-550899

Families Anonymous (Advice on family problems and drug abuse)
Unit 37
Dodington & Rollo Community Association
Charlotte Despard Avenue
London SW11 5JE
020-7498-4680

ACET (AIDS Advisers)
Central Office
PO Box 3693
London SW15 2BS
020-8780-0400

AGE Concern
Astral House
1268 London Road
London SW16 4ER
020-8679-8000

CRUSE Bereavement care
Cruse House
126 Sheen Road
Richmond
Surrey TW9 1UR
020-8940-4818

MIND (Advice on Mental Health)
020-8522-1728
0345-660-163

Relate (Marriage & Relationship Advice)
Herbert Gray College
Little Church Street
Rugby
CV21 3AP
01788-573-241

The Institute of Family Therapy (Therapeutic work with families and couples)
24–32 Stephenson Way
Euston
London NW1 2HX
020-7391-9150

The Samaritans (General Help-line)
0345-909-090
jo@samaritans.org

Survivors of Sexual Abuse
020-7890-4732